PRAISE FOR
The Secrets of Successful Co

"*The Secrets of Successful Communication* br... ...ly back into a world that depends so much on e-mails, texts, and tweets."
—Peter Hubbard, CEO, Pacific Title Archives

"This elegant message is just right for school and work. I want to have copies of the book for my clients. The book gets right to the point, and the examples are great. The best part is the Takeaways."
—William H. Crookston, Professor Emeritus of Clinical Enterpreneurship, USC Marshall School of Business

"Easy to read and filled with great examples, this book presents a thoughtful yet entertaining view of human communication . . . I believe everybody can take something from this book that will assist them to communicate better."
—Larry Applebaum, Member, Board of Education, Burbank Unified School District

"Kevin McCarney's book teaches how Big Brain communication impacts every aspect of our personal and business lives. The concepts in this book have assisted me in resolving some of the most difficult, hotly contested, and emotional lawsuits."
—Gig Kyriacou, Mediator, Kyriacou Mediation

"An easily digestible and important tool for those managing businesses or marriages. Kevin's keen observations detail both the pitfalls and successes of human interaction and how they can be improved upon."
—Lawrence Rudolph, Manager and Trainer, Pitfire Pizza Co.

"Simple and easy-to-use communication tools to help us relate better with those around us."
—Chelsea Holcomb, LCSW

"At home or in the office, *The Secrets of Successful Communication* is a valuable tool for improving the quality of life of readers and those around them. I am buying a copy for each of my 225 employees."
—Steve Supowitz, President, Individual FoodService

"I believe everyone needs a lesson in good communication skills for all types of relationships. *The Secrets of Successful Communication* is an absolute must-read for those who want to succeed in learning a true art form."
—Daniel A. Sanchez, Realtor, Dilbeck Realtors

"Kevin McCarney gets us back to the basics of how good interpersonal communications can benefit not only our professional lives but our most intimate relationships as well."
—Steven Schindler, Television Marketing Writer-Producer

"These communication principles can be effective with all cultures. This book should be part of everyone's customer service protocols."
—Barbara Gomperz, Entertainment Executive Director, International Sales and Operations

"A quick read, insightful and invaluable!"
—Mike Marmor, President, Emblem Enterprises, Inc.

"I have witnessed the success this book can bring in training both the owner and employees of a business."
—Frank Schwengel, Retired Small Business Lender and Advisor

Big Brain vs. Little Brain™ COMMUNICATION

THE SECRETS OF
Successful
COMMUNICATION

A SIMPLE GUIDE TO
EFFECTIVE ENCOUNTERS
IN BUSINESS

Kevin T. McCarney

O'Connell House
Toluca Lake, California

O'Connell House
10061 Riverside, #585
Toluca Lake, CA 91602

Ordering Information
Quantity sales. Special discounts are available on quantity purchases by corporations, associations, and others. For details, contact the "Special Sales Department" at the O'Connell House address above.

Individual sales. O'Connell House publications are available through most bookstores.

Orders by U.S. trade bookstores and wholesalers. Please contact Cardinal Publishers Group, 800-296-0481 or visit www.cardinalpub.com.

Cataloging-in-Publication data
McCarney, Kevin.
    The secrets of successful communication : a simple guide to effective encounters in business / Kevin McCarney.
        p. cm.
        Includes index.
        Series : Big Brain vs. Little Brain Communication
        ISBN 978-0-9831244-3-6
1. Business communication. 2. Communication in management. 3. Communication. 4. Oral communication. I. Series. II. Title.
HF5718 .M431
651.7/3—dc22   2011907053

Printed in the United States of America

FIRST EDITION
16 15 14 13 12 11   10 9 8 7 6 5 4 3 2 1

Cover design: Kuo Design
Design and type: Girl of the West Productions
Copyediting: PeopleSpeak

To Beatrice Jane McCarney,
my Big Brain mother with a heart to match.

And to my wife of twenty-three years, Nina,
and my daughters, Katelyn and Grace,
for their never-ending love and support.

CONTENTS

Preface   vii
Introduction: The Enchilada Story   1

Part One: Preparing for Effective Communication   **7**
  1 The Big Brain and the Little Brain   9
  2 Why Moments Matter   12
  3 Moments Create Legacies—Good or Bad   17
  4 The Circle of Influences   22
  5 Under the Influences   28
  6 The Biggest Influence on You Is You   32

Part Two: Encountering the Moment   **43**
  7 An Encounter—the Opening Act   45
  8 Big Brain and Little Brain in the Moment   49
  9 Every Conversation Is an Opportunity   54
  10 The Paradox of Communication Tools   61
  11 Managing Multiple Moments—the Social
        Media Effect   67
  12 Attack of the Little Brain—What You Can Do   73
  13 Big Brain and Little Brain—the Perpetual Race   77
  14 Finishing the Encounter   80
  15 What Legacies Are You Creating?   83

Part Three: Recognizing the Opportunities in the Moment   **87**

16   Awareness   89
17   Tone   96
18   Words   104
19   Control   112
20   Time   119
21   Responsibility   126
22   Power   132
23   Your Legacy Bank and Baggage   138

Part Four: Applying the Seven Principles of Big Brain
Communication   **143**

24   The First Principle: Stay Aware of the Legacy
     of the Moment   145
25   The Second Principle: Keep Your Big Brain
     in Control   149
26   The Third Principle: Choose the Correct *Tone*   152
27   The Fourth Principle: Choose the Correct Words   156
28   The Fifth Principle: Choose the Right Time   160
29   The Sixth Principle: Accept Responsibility   166
30   The Seventh Principle: Use Power Wisely   169

Afterword   173
Index   175
Acknowledgments   182
About the Author   185

PREFACE

Everyone is a people person. We are all in the people business.

Whether you are the leader of a Fortune 500 company, the leader of a family of five, a leader in your community, or just the leader of your own life, you encounter people every day, all day long. The quality of those encounters will determine your success in life.

You may not think of yourself as a people person, but just like you can't go swimming without getting wet, you can't be alive and not have encounters with other people. Whether we're walking down the street, answering a phone call, driving to work, texting, using Facebook, or tweeting, we are all interacting with people.

Virtually everything we do is some form of communication with others. Unfortunately, the art of communication has taken a backseat because we are all so busy that we don't always take the time to think before we communicate. Sometimes this causes problems. Sometimes it causes really big problems. But most importantly, sometimes it means we miss out on creating some great moments.

Barely a day goes by when we don't hear about how somebody somewhere said the wrong thing at the wrong time. Gaffes, "misspeaks," and misunderstandings are everywhere. People say, "Yes, that's what I said, but it's not what I meant to say."

Smart people, educated people, and even people with lots of experience speaking in public make mistakes when they are talking to others. Today, however, many of those mistakes are re-corded for others to hear or see. And the consequences of those mistakes have an impact on our families, our careers, and every other part of our lives.

Encounters

Life is filled with encounters. In the business world, those encoun-ters can be the determining factor in the success or failure of a business. In our personal lives, those encounters can mean the success or failure of our relationships.

This book is about how to make the most of each of those en-counters.

From boardrooms to restaurant dining rooms to encounters in everyday life, I have studied people's responses and reactions in hundreds of thousands of different situations and watched as the consequences of those reactions played out. My years of seeking to understand why people react the way they do have brought about the observations in this book.

Although many of the examples in this book involve work-places, when I set out to write *The Secrets of Successful Commu-nication*, I could not separate the workplace from the home. A workplace is made of individuals who come from home. And "employee" is just a label given to individuals at work. Putting on a suit or uniform does not strip away all of the influences in some-one's life. The way people respond and react in the workplace is often the same way they would act at home. Yes, we can put on a good front or even fake it for a little while, but ultimately our true communication skills will surface.

The reason we can't hide our true selves for very long is that many of our reactions and responses have a great deal to do with the events that are happening in our lives and how we are han-dling them. What is going on in our personal lives stays with us when we leave the house, and what happens on the job stays with us when we leave the workplace. Each environment can have an impact on our ability to communicate in the other.

Naturally Speaking

Our communication skills follow us everywhere we go. If we are to succeed at work and home, we need to improve our ability to speak with others no matter where we have an encounter.

What if there was a way to learn how to speak where it was natural to say the right thing at the right time, all the time, and just as natural to not say the wrong thing at the wrong time? We would have less need for damage control in our lives and have more pleasant lives all around.

This book offers solutions to many of today's most common communication issues. You will learn how to apply the principles in relationships, with your family, in your business life, and anywhere else you encounter people. Your natural way of speaking to others will improve, and your relationships will begin a new chapter of great communication.

*The real art of conversation is not only
to say the right thing at the right place
but to leave unsaid the wrong
thing at the tempting moment.*

DOROTHY FANNY NEVILL

INTRODUCTION
The Enchilada Story

The Enchilada Story is a true story that illustrates how simple responses in an everyday situation can change people's attitudes and reactions on the spot and turn an otherwise ugly moment into a friendly encounter with a positive outcome. Although it takes place at a restaurant, the lessons from the Enchilada Story are useful everywhere.

At a busy restaurant in the Westside of Los Angeles, two women walk in, stand in the long line, and wait for their turn to order. One of them orders a salad; the other, a plate of enchiladas. They find a table, and after a few minutes, the server brings their food with a smile and walks away.

Five minutes later, one of the women, let's call her Susan, returns to the counter and asks for the manager. The manager immediately walks over to greet her. Susan slams the plate of enchiladas on the counter and says in a very loud voice for all to hear, "These enchiladas are cold!"

The manager quickly responds, "I'm so sorry, I'll make you some new ones and get them out to you right away."

Susan walks back to her table angry.

Quickly the manager prepares a new order. Before the enchiladas leave the kitchen, he checks to make sure they are the right temperature. Begrudgingly, Susan accepts them.

1

Five more minutes pass. Susan comes back to the counter. "You made these enchiladas cold, too!" For a second the manager thinks he would be better off just giving Susan her money back and asking her to try something else. However, he keeps that thought to himself and says, "My sincere apologies. I will personally make you a new order, make sure they are hot, and bring them out to you myself."

Susan is still angry as she walks back to sit with her friend.

The manager makes the enchiladas. They are plate-meltingly hot when delivered. "Thank you so much for your patience," he says. "I assure you these will meet with your satisfaction."

Susan accepts the enchiladas with a sneer.

The restaurant is busy and the manager is distracted. After ten minutes go by, he looks over and notices that the enchiladas have not been touched. Concerned, he walks over to the table and says, "You know, maybe the enchiladas are not going to work for you today. Let me get you something else on the menu—anything. It's on me."

Susan, a little surprised, says, "Okay, get me some of those little round taquito things."

The manager gets them out quickly and delivers them personally. Susan accepts them.

Ten more minutes pass and the manager notices that Susan has touched only one of the three items. But before he can get over to her table, he gets busy with a long line of customers. As the lunch rush begins to wind down, the manager feels a hand on his arm. It is Susan.

She smiles at him and in a very sincere voice says, "Thank you."

"So, you liked the taquitos?"

"Oh, they were fine," Susan says, "but thank you for not getting angry at me. I am so sorry for the way I treated you. I'm exhausted from not sleeping. I just came from the hospital; my husband is not doing well, and there is nothing I can do. I don't know how to handle it, and I apologize for choosing you as the target of my frustration."

The manager replies, "I completely understand. Please don't give any thought to us."

Susan sighs. "Thank you again so much for not being upset."

The manager in a soft and concerned tone says, "I'm very sorry to hear about your husband. Thank you for sharing that with me. Please let me know if there is anything else I can do."

He and Susan trade smiles in a nonverbal acknowledgment of the lessons of the moment.

What are those lessons? Susan's reactions were never about the enchiladas; outside influences were driving this encounter. The manager, to his credit, did not take Susan's comments personally. Her comments were not personal; they were coming from influences that had nothing to do with the food, the service, or the situation.

After Susan left the restaurant, several customers who were there throughout the entire encounter went up to the manager and complimented him on the way he handled the moment. They indicated that the way he responded to Susan made *them* feel comfortable. When Susan apologized, they said, the whole experience made their day. They are still coming back to the restaurant, and so is Susan.

Lessons from the Enchiladas

Every day, in all areas of life, we find ourselves with choices in how we respond to a person or a situation. How we respond will have an immediate impact on us as well as a residual impact. We will be living with our choices long after we make them. But if we are aware of the outcome we want from a situation, it's easy to make the right choices in how we respond.

The biggest lesson of all—in any situation—is that it is not always about the "enchiladas" of the moment. Unseen influences can take over even the best of us, if only for a short time.

This book is for anyone who encounters people and who wants to make the most of those encounters. When it comes to having the ability to create great encounters, every moment counts.

Your business thrives with every great encounter, and it suffers with every poor one. The quality of the encounters your employees have with customers today will decide the future of your company tomorrow.

Your personal relationships are the same. They grow with every positive encounter, and they are injured by every negative encounter.

This book will help you identify the opportunities to turn every encounter into a great encounter. It provides some simple tools that will help you become a better ambassador of yourself and the businesses and organizations you're a part of.

You'll discover a precise yet simple and enjoyable method of learning to communicate effectively, positively, and even happily with everyone you encounter, from the angry customer who didn't get what he ordered to the noisy people sitting in front of you in the movie theater. The tools apply equally well to your private life as they do to your work life. The tips can work at home, at the office, at school, on the Little League diamond, and even on the freeway. The good news is that achieving the seemingly impossible result of outstanding communication with anyone is remarkably easy to teach, to learn, and to implement using the tools this book will share.

The book is organized into four parts. Part 1 unlocks the secrets of the two brains we all use in communication: the Big Brain and the Little Brain. You'll learn how to approach every communication moment in your day and create positive results. Part 2 breaks down the parts of an encounter and shows you how to have great conversations that will help you succeed in business and in your personal life. You'll find out what outside influences can affect what you say and how to spot when a client, a customer, or a friend is being influenced by factors that have nothing to do with you. You'll also learn how everything you say builds a legacy in the listener's mind.

In part 3 we'll take a closer look at those legacies and how you can improve them. What do people think about you? Do they remember you as someone who is classy, respectful, in control? Or do they think of you as someone who is disrespectful, whiny, or unfair? Do they see you as a calm, in-control leader or a hothead? What tools can you use to change their opinion for the better? What traps do you need to avoid? Along the way, stories about people in real-life situations—in business, in school, at home, or at a party—will illustrate the effects of both Big Brain and Little Brain reactions.

Finally, part 4 distills all these lessons into seven principles of Big Brain communication that you can use in every part of your life. Not only will these ideas build your own communication skills, but you can also share them with others. For example, maybe you're a manager whose front-line workers don't always make a great impression on customers or a teacher trying to help students develop communication skills that will help them get ahead in life. Or maybe you're a parent trying to communicate with children of any age. *The Secrets of Successful Communication* gives you simple, easy-to-remember ways to explain the art of communication to anyone—and become a better communicator yourself. Ready? Then let's meet "the man with two voices."

PART ONE

Preparing for
Effective Communication

"The Man with Two Voices." Sounds like the title of a science fiction movie from the fifties, doesn't it? You can almost see it playing on the screen in your mind—a man is walking down the street, seemingly normal, but he is speaking with two different voices, at times with a voice controlled by his Big Brain and at other times with a voice controlled by his Little Brain. Inside a nearby laboratory, two scientists are fighting over a control panel, battling to determine which of the brains will be in control of the man's next encounter.

When the scientist who controls the Big Brain wins, the man smiles, nods, and says the right thing to people. People like him. He's successful. Good things seem to follow him when he uses his Big Brain.

But when the scientist who wants the Little Brain to speak gets control, the man starts to frown and begins to make mean, irresponsible, and unfriendly statements to people. Bad things seem to be in his way, and they only get worse with every comment.

Although thousands of activities are actually going on in different parts of our brains at any given moment, the idea of the Big Brain and the Little Brain is used here to consolidate all of those actions into something most of us can easily understand. For our purposes, each of us has two brains we use to communicate, the Big Brain and the Little Brain.

These "communication brains" do not show up on a CAT scan. This concept is not based on how the synapses of the brain operate or on scientific studies of which part of the gooey stuff in our skulls is firing at any particular time. Instead, the Big Brain/ Little Brain concept is a way to help you think about how you communicate with other people.

We are all the same. Whether you're a millionaire or you're just starting your first job; whether you're single or married, a postgraduate or someone who did not finish high school; no matter your race, creed, or color; whether you're eight or eighty, this applies to you. When it comes to communication,

- We all have a Big Brain.
- We all have a Little Brain.
- We use them both every day.

The Big Brain and
the Little Brain

We all have a Big Brain. The Big Brain is all about responsibility, clear communications, thoughtful solutions, and long-term strategies. The Big Brain finds the right words to give the correct response in any situation.

Unfortunately, we also have a Little Brain. Our Little Brain is all about selfish comfort, indulgence, the need for power, carelessness, the inability to avoid problems, and short-term thinking. The Little Brain says and does the wrong thing at the wrong time.

When we engage with others using our Big Brain, things go well, people like us, and our relationships are successful. Everything is great at work. Everything is great at home.

When our Little Brain takes over, we cause problems for ourselves and everyone around us. Whether we're at home, at work, on the road, at events, or in any other situation, the Little Brain seems to seek out and embrace trouble.

Locations

Imagine that your Big Brain is located far away from your mouth. The Big Brain is the part of your reflective and thinking apparatus that allows you to carefully consider a situation and make an intelligent, diplomatic, successful choice every time you speak. The Big Brain, in short, is what keeps you focused, positive, and out of trouble. The Big Brain wants to get along with others and have successful and positive encounters every time. Its responses can take time to materialize and can lag behind the Little Brain's quick reactions because the Big Brain's responses travel a longer, more reflective path than the Little Brain's.

The Little Brain is located right next to the mouth and can't wait to spit out hasty, foolish, careless, embarrassing, sarcastic, cruel, or indifferent comments. The Little Brain has little regard for others. It just wants to say what it pleases at your expense and at the expense of almost everyone around you.

The Little Brain, because of its location, gets you in trouble. It doesn't think as deeply, so its reactions come out faster. Figure 1.1 shows the locations of the Big Brain and the Little Brain as discussed in this book.

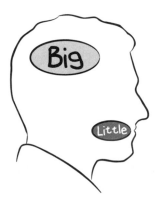

Figure 1.1 The Big Brain and the Little Brain

The Big Brain can be your best friend. The Little Brain can be your worst enemy.

When it comes to making sure that you are properly understood, the Big Brain is a champion. The Big Brain almost always suggests the words, tones of voice, and facial expressions that convey your best self—your warmth, your integrity, your desire to help others in any situation.

In any moment in life when you speak using guidance from the Big Brain, you communicate clearly and effectively. People understand what you're trying to say, and they appreciate not just the message but also the messenger.

CHAPTER TAKEAWAY

The Little Brain is impulsive and gets you into trouble. The Big Brain is thoughtful and allows you to grow. The key to being a great communicator is to use the Big Brain as often as possible and to find a way to prevent the Little Brain from causing trouble.

Why Moments Matter

Clearly, it's impossible to succeed if you allow your Little Brain to lead and control in your encounters with others. If your Little Brain says whatever it wants, is as nasty as it wants to be, and acts as hurtfully as it might like, people may never stick around long enough to get to know your Big Brain. They will, however, feel uncomfortable around you. Your family life will be strained, your coworkers won't be happy, your career could suffer, and your future will be less rewarding.

You're welcome to have Little Brain thoughts all day long. Nobody's going to take that away from you. But the question is whether you really think it's worth it to allow the petty desires and thoughts of your Little Brain to define you, your day, or your life.

Quite frankly, it's not fair to those around you to react from a Little Brain mentality. Your loved ones and your coworkers deserve better than that! They deserve the best of you.

They deserve the *Big Brain you* in every moment of your day.

Everyday Moments

Moments are our interactions with other people. When you wake up in the morning and greet your family, that's a moment. When you check Facebook and e-mail and communicate with others, those are all moments. When you get to work and interact with your coworkers and with your customers, those are moments. All these moments come together and become the experiences that make up your life.

Every day, life will present you with multiple opportunities to create great moments. As you pass people on the street, you will have chances to make otherwise insignificant moments significant. A moment may be opening a door for a person who obviously needs help or letting someone cut in front of you in line at the supermarket because you can see he is in a hurry. It could be smiling at a meter maid while she is giving a ticket. It could hinge on they way you speak to the counterperson at your local coffeehouse or how you engage with a coworker. It could even happen while you are driving to work. Your next moment is just around the corner.

Moments in Relationships

Far too often in our hectic, overscheduled lives, we don't notice the importance of moments as we pass through them. Learning to recognize the moments as they unfold is the only way to put our best selves into them and therefore get the best results from them.

Every day, we have a choice. Either we can pay attention to the moments that make up our lives, or we can live unconsciously through the day, unaware of what's really going on around us.

In each moment, we have a choice as well. We can keep our Big Brain in control, or we can allow our Little Brain to be activated and lose control.

In every relationship, the bond between two people is constantly changing. The energy in the relationship is being either improved or harmed. How? The manner in which the two individuals communicate with and act toward each other in any given moment creates either positive energy or negative energy.

In other words, your relationship with another person is actually a long series of connected moments. The more conscious you are of these moments, the more likely you are to build a closer, more positive relationship with that person.

Career Moments

The same principles apply in the workplace. The greatest problem that businesses face today has less to do with the economy and competition than it does with keeping the customers and clients they already have and attracting new ones. We need to remember that many new customers come as referrals from the customers we already have. The customer in front us is our most valuable resource.

The front-line people—the individuals who actually greet and serve customers—must always recognize the importance of the moments they share with their customers and coworkers. If they're too busy talking with each other to give a sincere hello to a customer, his reaction is likely to be, "I don't think I'm going to receive good service here." Not only the lack of a good greeting but the experience of a poor greeting—basically *being ignored*—may lead him to turn around and leave.

A business that treats customers like this is losing market share one customer at a time. Actually, it is losing more than one customer because unhappy customers not only tell their friends but also go online and tell the world, sometimes while they are still in the store.

In the moment when a customer is dealing with a front-line person of a company, that person becomes the face of the company. She becomes the Marketing Department, Advertising Department, and Customer Service Department of the entire company for that customer for that moment.

Business owners and managers are often shocked when they visit a website like Yelp, Google Maps, or any other site that offers customer reviews of businesses. They can't believe how negative some of the comments are. Their typical reaction can be Little Brain itself—"Who do these people think they are? They're so rude! I don't even want them for customers! They're just crazy!"

Those business owners and managers are missing the point. The individuals making these comments aren't nuts. They're people who *were already in their stores*, people who chose to do business with them. However, a front-line person (the salesclerk, server, hotel clerk, phone operator, or whoever) failed to recognize the importance of the moment. That person failed to welcome the customer properly, failed to stop chatting, or failed to simply take a moment to make eye contact and say hello.

You don't want your name or your business's name in a negative comment left on a blog. If you want to have a successful career, it's up to you to recognize the importance of moments both to you and to your company. Every single interaction with a customer is a moment. The stronger the moment is the stronger the company, the safer your position, and the greater the likelihood of growth and advancement.

Recognizing opportunities to welcome and greet new or returning customers and helping people get what they want will turn those customers into repeat visitors and ambassadors of goodwill for you and your business. *The core mission of every successful business is to inspire customers to return.*

Mopping Moments

In addition, every moment with a coworker will have an impact on your ability to grow within in your company. Your interactions— your moments with coworkers—no matter how brief or seemingly insignificant, can have far longer-term significance than you realize.

For example, a teenager had a summer job mopping the floors of the Pepsi-Cola bottling plant in Long Island, New York, near his home. He was determined to be the best at whatever job he was doing, even if the only job he could get that summer was mopping floors. His boss noticed how efficient and hardworking he was over the course of the summer. The two did not speak all that often, but by the end of the summer, the boss thought enough of the teen's diligence at mopping floors and working with others that he made sure to tell him to come back to work the next summer.

The following summer the young man returned to get a job, but instead of mopping floors, he was promoted to the bottling machine. By the end of that summer he was a deputy shift supervisor—all because he mopped floors so well that he created enough positive moments to impress the boss, and that opened up more opportunities for him.

Who was the young man? You might have heard of him: Colin Powell, who went on to be the first African American chairman of the Joint Chiefs of Staff and United States secretary of state.

Even seemingly unimportant moments that occur when you think no one is watching can put you on the road to important success. How you respond, how you behave, and the words and tone you choose can have an extremely powerful effect on your career and on your life.

Moments don't last that long. So why are they so important? It is because of what they leave behind.

CHAPTER TAKEAWAY

You are always creating moments. Every day brings dozens of opportunities to create moments that will make a difference in your life and the lives of others. The choice is yours as to what kind of moment you want to create, and as Colin Powell's experience shows, someone is always watching.

Moments Create Legacies— Good or Bad

So far we've discussed the Big Brain, the Little Brain, and moments. We've seen that when we use our Big Brain, we create positive moments for ourselves and for those around us at home, at work, or wherever we go. When we use our Little Brain, we get the opposite results. The kind of moment you create is important long after the moment is over. But if moments last only, well, a moment, why are they so important?

Because moments create legacies.

When you interact with someone and the moment ends, what is left behind is the legacy of that moment. It is the impression the moment leaves with the other person. It is your reputation, positive or negative. It is how you will be remembered. The next time you see that person, your legacy from that last encounter will be present.

If you interact in a Big Brain fashion, you create a positive legacy for that moment. Positive moments make people like you. When people like you, they look forward to seeing you, they like being in relationship with you, and they like working with you. They tell their friends how wonderful you are. You begin to build trust and friendships.

By contrast, when you allow your Little Brain to dictate the terms of a moment, you create a negative legacy. A negative legacy can lead to people not liking you, not looking forward to seeing you, not wanting to do work with you, or even ending a relationship with you.

How to Create Positive Legacies

No matter how difficult or challenging the other person might be or how difficult the circumstances are, you can create a positive legacy. And you can learn how to turn existing negative legacies positive by improving your people skills with some tools that we will identify later in the book.

Leaving a positive Big Brain legacy creates future opportunities. Leaving a negative Little Brain legacy creates future problems, ditches to dig yourself out of, and obstacles to overcome.

The ability to leave the legacy you desire comes down to fine-tuning your people skills. There are many forms of people skills, but we'll look at the ones that make it easier to understand others and to be understood.

People skills are simpler than a lot of people think. It is important to

- Respond from your Big Brain and not react from your Little Brain.
- Truly listen to what is being said. Be in the moment.
- Be aware that every interaction with another human being is a moment and you have the power to make that moment positive or negative.
- Recognize that every moment creates a legacy and the legacy dictates how people feel about you, their relationship with you, and whether they want you in their future.

So the question is, When you are in a situation with another human being, which part of you gets activated most of the time: the Big Brain or the Little Brain? To see what a difference that can make, let's look at the nail-biting finish of a Little League season.

A Little League team, like any business or organization, is part family and part business. Everyone is striving for the goal of winning the game, but because of how much time the people spend together, they become a family of coworkers, a team. A strong team leader will begin to observe and encourage people's growth as individuals as well as the team's growth. In many ways, how any team is coached will mean the difference between success in keeping the team together and focused or the failure to be effective and to hold onto good people. Every team leader experiences moments of pressure that define that leader. Those moments have legacies, as the following story illustrates.

Big Brain and Little Brain in Action: The Final Game

It is the ninth inning of a league championship, and the Generals are up to bat. They are behind by two runs with two outs and one runner on third. At bat is Jeff, the best hitter on the team. Jeff hits the ball deep into left field for a hit, and everyone is running. The runner on third easily makes it home. If Jeff makes it home, he will score the tying run. As he rounds second he can see that the ball will beat him to home plate, but the coach is waving him in. Jeff hesitates, just for a second, and is thrown out at the plate. The Generals lose the game.

The coach's response can go in one of two different directions: a Little Brain reaction or a Big Brain response. Let's look at a Little Brain reaction first.

Little Brain Reaction

Jeff walks to the dugout. From his place in front of the dugout, the coach of the Generals is screaming at Jeff for hesitating: "Did you see the sign?" When Jeff responds with a yes, the coach replies, "Well, you lost us the game."

Jeff is now in tears, but the parents stay silent, enabling the coach's bad behavior. The coach walks back to the dugout, yelling at everyone in front of him and pushing equipment to the side.

In an effort to change the mood, one of the parents calls out, "Okay, everyone, let's get to the after party," and the coach says, "I'll be there later . . . if I get a chance."

The whole team is feeling down as the players walk to their cars.

What's the legacy of this type of reaction? The next season, most of the players do not come back. The turnover really hurts the team, and the Generals, with the same coach, have a very poor season.

Now let's look at how a leader using his Big Brain would handle the situation.

Big Brain Response

Jeff walks to the dugout. The coach gives Jeff a pat on the shoulder and tells him it's okay. Jeff is down and feels totally responsible. The coach asks all the players and their families to move down the sidelines into left field. The screams of joy of the winning team can still be can be heard as the coach of the Generals begins to speak.

"Well, boys, this was a great game and a great season, and I am very proud of you. We took a great shot and we did our best. You all played great today, and I want you to hold your heads high." He looks directly at Jeff. "Jeff, that was a great hit, and I should not have waved you in. That was my fault. I got a little excited. I am sorry to the whole team for making that decision."

Jeff says, "I could have run faster."

The coach replies, "The ball was too far ahead of you and you saw that. I made the bad call."

One of the parents responds, "Hey, it's baseball."

"This is not the end of the season," the coach continues. "We have an after party that we will all attend and celebrate the great things that have happened this year. Each one of you has my deep admiration for your hard work this season. I hope you all feel good about what you have done this year, and I will make a commitment to being here next year so we can win the whole thing. Now let's get some food and have some fun."

The mood lightens and some laughs are [...] walk to their cars.

What's the legacy? The next year, all the pla[...] they begin to work better as a team. They have o[...] seasons in the team's history.

In a moment of pressure, the coach took the opport[...] accept responsibility and to let everyone know that it was a[...] the team and not his ego. The following year he did not lose a si[...] gle team member. His words inspired all the players to be proud of what they had done and to look forward to the new season.

What's Happening?

Let's take a step back and ask, What activates the Big Brain and what activates the Little Brain? What influences are brought to bear every time we have an encounter with others, especially those encounters when we are under pressure? We must first understand the current influences in our lives and how they play a part in activating the Big Brain or the Little Brain.

CHAPTER TAKEAWAY

What we leave behind doesn't stay in the past. It is actually in front of us in the future. It's the legacy of the moment. Your legacy is the residual impact of your communications and your actions. Such impacts will come back to you as opportunities or obstacles when you have future encounters.

heard as the players

vers return and

e of the best

nity to

bout

n-

fluences

When you regret saying something the minute the words leave your mouth, you will often sit back and think, "What was I thinking?" or "Why did I say that?" The cause is often something subtle happening in your life—influences that you cannot see and may not even be aware of.

What are the influences that cause you to come from either your Big Brain or your Little Brain? The first indicator is your initial response or reaction.

First Response

Your initial response in any situation is the most critical because it sets the tone and direction of the encounter and the moments that follow. At this point, the Little Brain and the Big Brain begin to struggle to see which will respond. It's here where the influences in your life will begin to have an impact on your choice.

The dictionary indicates that "influence" is a *compelling force that affects someone's actions or thoughts.* For our purposes, an influence is the *motivation* behind what can pull you or push you into a Little Brain or Big Brain state. It also has the power to affect what you say. So the question is this: When you have encounters with other human beings, what is the compelling force that affects the way you act?

Figure 4.1 introduces the Big Brain and Little Brain influences as wedge shapes. Ultimately these wedges form a *Circle of Influences*, which you will see a bit later in this chapter. When an influence is in Big Brain mode, it is shown in white with black letters; when in Little Brain mode, it shown in gray with black letters.

Figure 4.1 Influences

The Influences

Many things can become influences on us. The key influences that affect our Big Brain responses and our Little Brain reactions are primal influences, surrounding influences, career and financial influences, and situational influences:

- Primal influences deal with how we feel in both our bodies and minds.
- Surrounding influences come from the people in our lives.
- Career and financial influences come from fiscal and future outlook impacts.
- Situational influences deal with circumstances in our lives.

Primal Influences

Primal influences (fig. 4.2) result from the physical or emotional feelings we are having:

- Physical comfort influences might include, for example, being hungry or thirsty, too hot or too cold, tired or energetic. Being ill or on medication (prescription or otherwise) can also influence physical comfort.

- Emotional comfort influences would be how we feel at a particular moment—for example, happy or sad, loving or hateful, fearful or brave.

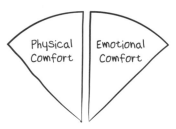

Figure 4.2 Primal influences

Surrounding Influences

Surrounding influences (fig. 4.3) are the people in our lives:

- Family influences might include a spouse, a partner, parents, siblings, an aunt, or an uncle.
- Friends/relationships might include a girlfriend, a boyfriend, old friends, or new friends.

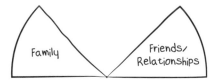

Figure 4.3 Surrounding influences

Career and Financial Influences

Career and financial influences (fig. 4.4) are how we make a living and support ourselves:

- Work/school influences might include our coworkers, teachers, or boss.

- Money/finances might involve mortgage or rent, tuition, car payments, or insurance.

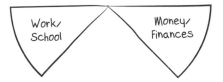

Figure 4.4 Career and financial influences

Situational Influences

Situational influences (fig. 4.5) result from the immediate circumstances in our lives:

- Public situations might occur, for example, in traffic, at the movie theater, in parking lots, at events, in restaurants, and the like.
- Time influences can include daily time pressures, deadlines, meetings, reports to write, and more.

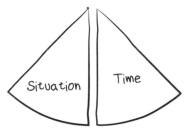

Figure 4.5 Situational influences

Putting the Pieces Together

Figure 4.6 shows what it looks like when we put all the pieces together. They form a large Circle of Influences. Each influence can be in either Big Brain mode or Little Brain mode.

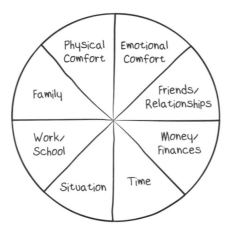

Figure 4.6 The Circle of Influences

Any one of these areas or any combination of them has the ability to put us in a Big Brain or in a Little Brain state on any particular day or at any particular moment. Many of us don't pay attention to these influences, and we end up paying the price because when we're stressed in any area of our life and we aren't aware of how stressed we are, our Little Brain can get activated. When we use it instead of our Big Brain, we cause trouble.

What about you? Are you aware of the various influences that dictate what kind of mode you're in at any given time? Keeping all of your influences in Big Brain mode is no easy task, but with practice it will become simpler and more fun.

The Enchilada Story Revisited

Let's take a look back at the Enchilada Story and break it down to illustrate how the Circle of Influences was impacting the way Susan reacted. She was experiencing some difficulties in her life:

- "I'm exhausted from not sleeping"—Her physical comfort influence was in Little Brain mode.
- "My husband is not doing well"—Her family influence was in Little Brain mode.

- "There is nothing I can do"—Her emotional comfort influence was in Little Brain mode.

Susan's husband was very ill, and she felt that she did not have any control in her life, which added to her emotional discomfort. Without realizing it, she exerted her power in the one place she felt she could. She used the enchiladas as a way to deal with some powerful influences.

CHAPTER TAKEAWAY

Most of the time, we aren't even aware of the influences that drive us. In the last interaction you had with another person, what influences were most dominant and impacted how you spoke? What are the influences in your life right now?

Under the Influences

Sometimes influences can hijack your more thoughtful responses and replace them with reactions that you later regret and blame on impulse, emotion, or other people. That's when you find yourself saying, "Uh-oh, that was not what I wanted to say." That was your Little Brain.

When you interact with others, you are constantly being influenced to make a choice between using your Big Brain and using your Little Brain. It may not seem like it in the moment, but you always have a choice. Even though several influences may be present in any particular encounter and some may seem to have more power than others, they do not have the final say in what you are going to say or how you are going to say it. It is always your choice whether you allow the influences to control you or you control the influences on your responses.

Simply put, when your influences are in Big Brain mode, they bring intelligence and diplomacy to any situation. Your Big Brain has a great attitude, always sees the best in people, and avoids trouble by saying and doing the right thing pretty much every time. That's regardless of whether other people are using their Little Brains and treating you well or not.

Your Little Brain, by contrast, has a big mouth!

To see how this process works, let's take a closer look at influences in an everyday situation.

Big Brain and Little Brain in Action: A Long Day

Mary has had a trying day at work. She's a dental hygienist, and today she was overscheduled with patients. In the middle of the day, with the waiting room filled with people, the office's computer system failed. Mary and the office receptionist worked like mad to keep the appointments flowing smoothly, but inevitably, things got backed up, and Mary felt the full force of her patients' irritation after they'd been kept waiting forty-five minutes or longer. She did not take her normal lunch just to keep things moving.

When she finally leaves work and heads to the kindergarten to pick up her son, Sam, she's feeling tired, worn out, and hungry. Sam, on the other hand, has had a grand day. His teacher showed the class how to use construction paper and magazine clippings to make a collage, and he is eager to show his mother his project.

Immediately after Mary has Sam buckled into the backseat and gets behind the wheel, he starts calling, "Mommy! Mommy! Look in my backpack!"

Mary is thinking how much she wants to get home, have something to eat, and relax. She has already started the car and is pulling away from the curb and into traffic—she can't drive and rummage around in Sam's backpack at the same time. She feels herself tense, but suddenly her Big Brain kicks in and she realizes she has a choice in how she responds to Sam.

She could say curtly, "Sam, I need you to sit still and be quiet right now. I can't look in your backpack and drive at the same time." That would quiet him down quickly and allow her to get home faster after her long day. But Sam has no idea what Mary's been dealing with today; he's just excited about his project and wants to share that excitement with his mom. What if Mary did shut him down? His child's mind would have a hard time grasping the outside influences Mary is under, and he might think that her reaction is his fault or that he did something wrong.

Instead, Mary takes a moment and chooses to explain, "Sam, I bet you've got something really special to show me, and I can't wait to see it. But I can't take a good look at what you have done while I'm driving, so how about we wait until we get home?"

Mary's first reaction would have been a Little Brain one: quick, thoughtless, and ultimately negative. All she has to do is pause and evaluate a split second longer, and her Big Brain kicks in with the thoughtful, appropriate, and positive response that Sam needs and appreciates.

Think about this situation. As figure 5.1 shows, Mary's *primal physical comfort influences* were in Little Brain mode: she was tired and hungry. She was under the *time influence* of wanting to get home. Her *career influences* of work were partly in Little Brain mode, too: she had dealt with cranky patients all day. However, she also had the positive help of the office receptionist in dealing with the IT crisis. And at the end of the day, she had the positive, Big Brain family influence of her son, Sam. Finally, she was dealing with the Little Brain *situational influence* of having had a long, hard day at work and then driving through traffic but also the Big Brain *emotional comfort influence* of wanting to share an important

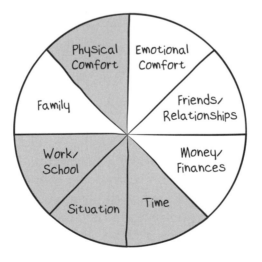

Figure 5.1 Mary's influences in the moment

project with her son. As you saw, even with all these influences in Little Brain mode, Mary was capable of choosing a Big Brain response instead of a Little Brain reaction.

We all know that driving under the influence is bad because it can cause accidents and hurt people. What we don't realize is that in some moments we are "living under the influence." Our responses, even our behavior, is constantly being influenced by a wide variety of factors. So why do you at times react from your Little Brain? What are the influences in your life? How do they impact you? We need to pay attention to one more influence. And it's the biggest influence of all. You can find it staring back at you in the mirror.

CHAPTER TAKEAWAY

We don't just choose randomly between our Big Brain and our Little Brain at any given moment. There's almost always a reason, an influence, as to why we respond from our Big Brain or react from our Little Brain. Despite the influences that are present, we always have a choice.

The Biggest Influence
on You Is You

Socrates said it best: "Know Thyself." A wide range of influences affects you every day. And yet, even if many of your influences are in Little Brain mode on a particular day, your sense of personal "self" will have the final power over your responses. Your core sense of self-image and self-respect and your overriding sense of self-confidence in who you are will often decide which brain will respond or react.

When you combine all of these core senses of self, they form your sense of Me. This is not a selfish Me, not an arrogant Me, and not a greedy Me—but a personal Me. This is who I am, and this is how I feel about Me today.

As figure 6.1 shows, your core self-esteem, what we call your Me, comprises your self-image, self-confidence, self-respect, belief/religion, and values.

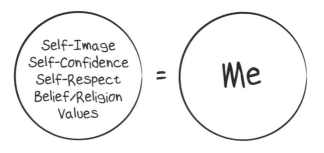

Figure 6.1 Your core self-esteem

How you are feeling about who you are at any particular moment affects the ability of other influences to push or pull you to choose a Big Brain response or a Little Brain reaction.

Although primal, surrounding, career and financial, and situational influences are the ones you need to be aware of as you enter a particular encounter, other major influences can have a powerful impact on your Me and can override any other influence. These can have either major positive or major negative impacts. What are these major influences? They are big events or big changes in your life beyond your normal routine, beyond the normal influences, and often beyond your control.

Major Influences That Impact Your Me

Any major change or event in your life has the potential to impact your Me. If the change is positive, your Me can gain strength, your path and direction can become clearer, and you can feel more in control.

On the other hand, if the change takes you out of your normal confident, self-assured Me, it can cause a sense of "Who am I? What am I doing?" you can begin to doubt yourself, and a feeling of a weak Me can take over.

For example, if you are in the middle of a breakup with a partner, if you just lost your job or just started a new one, or if you have to move to a new neighborhood, go to a new school, or make some other major change in your life, your Me is potentially weakened. If you make a mistake, and we all do from time to time, and you have not dealt with it yet, the guilt can be a major influence until it is resolved. Circumstances like these can leave you more vulnerable to outside influences.

Your Me is weakened the same way your immune system can be weakened, making it easier to become ill. Ralph Waldo Emerson had it right when he said, "If I have lost confidence in myself, I have the universe against me."

If, though, you just started dating someone, moved out on your own for the first time, received an award for a job well done, got a promotion, or added to your family, your Me will be very strong, and outside influences do not stand a chance of pushing you into Little Brain mode.

It's like having an immune system that has been strengthened by proper diet, exercise, attitude, and rest. Disease and illness have less of a chance to take hold.

Taking Control, Having a Choice

You can't always control the major events in your life, but you still have a choice in your response to them. If your Me gets weakened, rebuilding and maintaining a strong Me may take a while, but once you accomplish this, you can properly respond to the influences around you. Most major incidents or changes in your life, whether they are emotional or circumstantial, take time to work themselves out. They take time to process. During this time you need to keep your Little Brain from taking advantage of the situation and keep your Big Brain in control.

Your Me is your strongest influence when you communicate. When your core sense of Me is strong, you can fend off multiple Little Brain influences around you and still respond in Big Brain mode. But when your core sense of self-esteem is weak, it does not take much to push you into a Little Brain reaction. Later on we will discuss tools that will keep your Me strong and even strengthen it with each response.

A strong Me (fig. 6.2) will act as a powerful barrier that does not allow Little Brain influences to penetrate and impact your responses.

Strong Me

Some days you may have more than a single influence in Little Brain mode. When that happens, your ability to keep from blurting out a Little Brain comment depends on the strength of your Me.

Figure 6.2 A strong Me

We have all heard the expression "having a bad day." Figure 6.3 shows what a bad day looks like when there are multiple Little Brain influences. In this example, only one influence is in Big Brain mode. Figure 6.4 shows a strong Me with multiple Little Brain influences on a bad day.

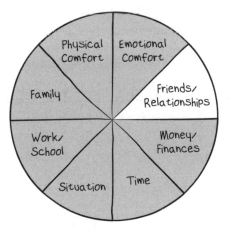

Figure 6.3 The Circle of Influences on a bad day

However, figure 6.5 shows that even with most of the influences in a Little Brain mode, a strong Me can keep them all in perspective and produce a Big Brain response.

A strong Me can strengthen your ability to handle anything.

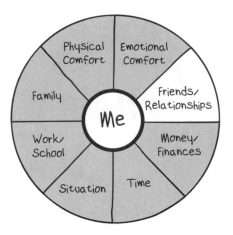

Figure 6.4 Strong Me under pressure

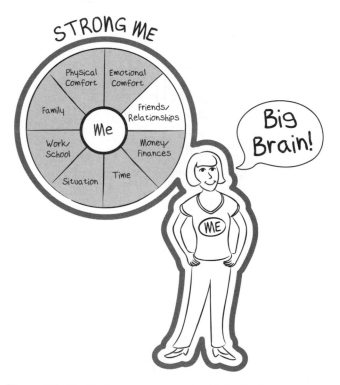

Figure 6.5 Big Brain response under Little Brain pressure

On the other hand, a weak Me (fig. 6.6) will act as an open barrier that allows Little Brain influences to penetrate and take over your reactions.

Weak Me

When your Me is weak, it leaves you open to outside influences affecting your reactions. When this occurs, even though many other influences can be in Big Brain mode, a single influence can sometimes result in a Little Brain reaction.

Figure 6.7 illustrates a person with all but one influence in Big Brain mode.

If you know your Me is weakened by a major influence, you can slow down your reactions to keep your Little Brain from taking advantage of the situation. The extra time will allow your Big Brain to kick in and prevent a poor reaction. Figure 6.8 shows a weak Me on an otherwise good day with just two Little Brain influences.

Let's take a closer look at the weak Me. Figure 6.9 illustrates what happens when your Me is weak and how one influence in Little Brain can bring upon a Little Brain reaction. A weak Me can leave you vulnerable to make a Little Brain comment.

Let's see how that works in this story.

Figure 6.6 A weak Me

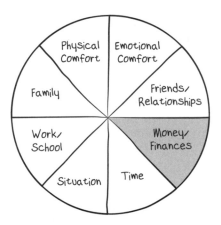

Figure 6.7 Circle of Influences on a good day

Big Brain and Little Brain in Action: Hitting a Sour Note

The music shop where Patrick works as a salesman and teaches guitar lessons is struggling. The owner had to cut back on hours, and yesterday he called Patrick into his office to let him know that he didn't have enough students registered to continue offering guitar lessons.

Patrick is devastated. Teaching guitar is what he loves most about his job. As a musician, he has always had a difficult time making a living doing what he loves, and when he took the job as a salesman, he told himself that he was still staying connected to his craft by teaching. The moment Patrick had that meeting with his boss, he started to wonder if the cutbacks were really about the shop's financial situation. He began to doubt his talent and himself.

"Maybe that's just a cover," Patrick thinks. "Maybe my boss is cutting back on my lessons because I'm just not a good teacher or guitar player." His Me is suffering.

With his weakened Me, it's suddenly not very hard for Patrick to slip into Little Brain reactions. Toward the end of the day,

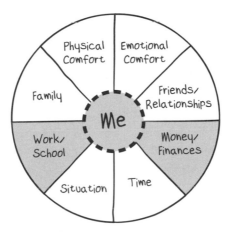

Figure 6.8 Weak Me under pressure

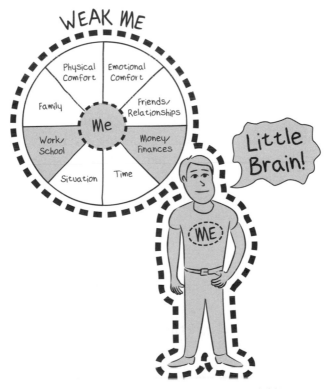

Figure 6.9 Little Brain reaction to a weak Me

preoccupied with his disappointment, Patrick is stocking guitar strings at the back of the store when a customer approaches him.

"Do you sell mandolins?" the customer wants to know.

Patrick doesn't want to be bothered. "Do you see any mandolins? No, you don't. That's because we don't have any." That is an answer straight from his Little Brain (see fig. 6.9).

The customer is taken aback and stands there for a moment, waiting to see if Patrick will offer any other advice. But Patrick just continues stocking the strings and ignores him. Eventually, the customer leaves—and tells his friends that not only is Patrick's store understocked but also that its salespeople are rude.

If Patrick hadn't allowed his weakened Me to affect his reaction, his response might have come from his Big Brain. He might have said, "We don't carry mandolins in the store, actually. But if there's a particular model you're interested in, we can order it for you from our distributor. Do you want to take a look at the catalogue?"

The customer would have left feeling satisfied and appreciated, and Patrick would have started to slowly reenergize his Me by investing his energies in the vocation and job he loves—music. Eventually, when the store got out of its sales slump, he'd even have a good shot at going back to teaching guitar lessons.

Every day, some moments may throw you off guard and you can begin to play out many different scenarios as to why something was done or was not done. During these times, your Little Brain can be very active. That's when your Big Brian will help you focus on moving forward with a positive outlook until your questions are answered.

So now that you know about Big Brain/Little Brain, moments, legacies, and influences, how do they come into your life? How do they affect you? Through the encounters you experience every day.

CHAPTER TAKEAWAY

Knowing whether your Me is strong or weak on any particular day is critical. The biggest influence on choosing between your Little Brain and your Big Brain isn't something outside you. It's you yourself. It's your Me. Your Me will have the final say in your say.

PART TWO

Encountering the Moment

As we have seen, our lives are full of moments. Every moment begins with an encounter. An encounter is the "opening act" of each new interaction, each new moment. You can visualize an encounter as having four parts (fig. II.1). First you meet someone, receive a message, or make a call. Now the moment opens: you

1. Encounter	2. Moment Opens

You receive a message
You meet with someone
You make a call
You have a chance
  encounter
	A conversation begins
	A dialogue develops
	An exchange of
	  comments occurs

3. Choice	4. Legacy

You make a choice:
 	
  Big Brain response
      or
  Little Brain reaction
	You leave behind the
	lasting consequences
	of the moment

Figure II.1 The parts of an encounter

begin a conversation and exchange comments. Next you have a choice of a Big Brain response or a Little Brain reaction. The final part of an encounter is the encounter's legacy, the lasting consequences of the moment.

An Encounter—
the Opening Act

In our daily travels, we interact with many people under different circumstances. At home, an encounter starts when we greet our loved ones. At work, it begins when we first notice a coworker or customer. Ideally, we seize the opportunity to create a positive moment. A passing smile, the simple touch of a hand, or even eye contact can be a meaningful encounter.

We encounter people on the way to work, on the street, on the highway, in restaurants, in malls, at events, and in so many other ways. Even listening to the radio in the car is an encounter. The dialogue may be happening in your mind, but nevertheless, there is an exchange of thoughts. On an average day, you might have twenty to thirty or more encounters. Some people, depending on their jobs, may have thirty different encounters by noon.

You know the wonderful feeling you experience when you're greeted warmly when you step into a store, a restaurant, or any place that serves the public. And you know the vaguely unhappy, insulted feeling you get when you're ignored. We go back to the places that make us feel comfortable, and we stay away from the ones that do not.

Think of someone working at the checkout stand of a supermarket. She will have dozens of encounters with people each day. She might be the only person in the store with whom customers actually speak. That's a heavy responsibility. The way she encounters customers—whether she offers a warm greeting or just stares solemnly at the food as she rings it up—will dictate, to a large degree, how customers feel about their entire shopping experience at that particular store. For the supermarket, a lot is riding on the moments created in these encounters.

Even if your routine is the same day after day and you are interacting not with the general public but with coworkers at your company, new encounters will present themselves each day. Think about today. Reflect back to this morning and identify the places you were, the people with whom you interacted, and the things you heard and learned as you spoke with others. Start with the first person you saw after you woke up.

If you'd like, take a moment and write down as many encounters as you can recall. You might be surprised just how many encounters you have with other human beings each day!

An encounter creates the opportunity for a moment to open. No matter where the encounter takes place, the quality of the encounter—which is up to you—is determined by the quality of the moments. The better the moments that you create, the more success you will enjoy. Your response during your encounters will form the legacies that make up your life. Some encounters are ones that we can see on a calendar and plan for. Others happen suddenly and without notice.

Perfect Game, Perfect Encounter, Perfect Legacy

Every day we see people who are under extreme pressure from different influences in their lives and are still able to respond with their Big Brain when communicating with others.

One example is pitcher Armando Galarraga, who was on his way to pitching a perfect game—only to have the umpire make a bad call on the last out of the last inning. The call to the rest of the world and to Galarraga was easy. The runner at first was out. Instant replay proved what everyone knew: the runner was out. But the umpire had called him safe, taking away one of the most prized achievements in all of baseball: the perfect game. Only eighteen perfect games have been pitched in modern baseball history.

The enormity of the event set the media on fire. It seemed for a while that the entire sports world wanted revenge.

The umpire felt terrible and even he himself could not believe that he had made the call. The airways were filled with people who wanted the decision reversed, and what they were saying about the umpire was downright mean.

In a game known for foul language and physical outbursts, Galarraga did not buy into the anger of others or the sadness at losing his spot in history. He did not join in the name-calling. He seemed to understand, more than most, that bad calls happen in baseball and you move on. The umpire asked Galarraga to come to the umpire's room. The umpire had been crying, and his body language spoke more than his words. That is when Galarraga gave him a hug of forgiveness.

At the most unexpected time, in a difficult encounter, in one of the most emotional moments in all of baseball, Galarraga pitched a Big Brain response and secured himself a place in baseball history. That is a strong Me.

What was the legacy of this response? The next day, Galarraga received a brand-new Corvette in front of all the fans for the sportsmanship he showed in the way he handled the situation. The Baseball Hall of Fame asked for his spikes and for the first-base bag from the infamous play to place in its museum along with the story of the moment. Instead of being on the bottom of a list of nineteen, Gallaraga would be at the top of a list of his own.

So where do you go from here? How do you make every encounter turn into a positive moment? Read on.

CHAPTER TAKEAWAY

Every encounter is an opportunity to make a good choice. A positive encounter sets the stage for positive, Big Brain–driven, successful moments and legacies.

Big Brain and Little Brain in the Moment

So often, we fail to take the time to live in the moments. We move so fast and take on so much that when we simply get through the day, we feel we have accomplished something. All too often, we miss many opportunities to enrich our lives and the lives of others along the way.

A moment, you will recall, is an interaction, the back and forth between you and another human being, whether at work, at home, on the highway, or anywhere else. *The quality of your moments determines the quality of your life.* The quality of the moments with friends and family are the ones that have the greatest impact on your life. The quality of your moments at work will dictate how well you're going to do in your career.

All Day, Every Day

From the time you open your eyes in the morning until you close them at night, you are in a series of moments. Most moments pass with little to no consequence. But hidden in the middle of those inconsequential moments are the ones that shape your life for good or for bad.

We seldom realize that each moment has the power to create great feelings or bad feelings for the person with whom we are interacting. If we aren't consciously aware that a moment is an opportunity, we could interact with that person with our Little Brain. And you know how much trouble that can cause.

We create hundreds of sentences and dozens of conversations that make up the moments of our day. Everyone is different, but most of us speak or write between four thousand and eight thousand words each day. But how many times are we actually thinking about the words we use or how we are saying them? How many times are we truly engaged in the conversation, and how many times are we just repeating words we have heard before to fill the silence between exchanges?

Every conversation is a new moment opened. It's like creating a new file on your computer. What are you going to put into that file? How will the other person label that file—as a positive moment or a negative moment? It's up to you!

Little Brain Happens

We all have Little Brain moments. There is no way to completely stop the Little Brain from occasionally getting in a crude comment, a bad joke, or a poorly timed release of information. You are not alone. It happens to everyone, and usually there is no cause for alarm. Just recognize that you have had a Little Brain moment and think about what may have activated your Little Brain.

If you were among close friends who treated your Little Brain comment as insignificant, then let it go. You don't have to try to be perfect. No one is.

If it was a significant remark that will cause a poor legacy, don't panic. You can go back and fix it using some of the legacy tools we will describe a little later.

The same rule applies when you are confronted with Little Brain moments created by others in your daily life: most are not significant, and you can let them pass without comment or response. If you do feel a need to say something, be sure the comment is coming from your Big Brain. Many times, a Big Brain response would be to not waste time making a fuss about someone else's Little Brain activity. Sometimes it is a good idea just to move on.

Big Brain, Big Moment

Big Brain moments happen all day long. You may not always take the time to recognize them, but they are there. Think of all the courtesy that has been extended to you over the last year, month, week, or several days. Ponder the situations in which someone made you more comfortable by using the right tone or the right words for the circumstances. Think of all the times you have witnessed Big Brain moments. Here's an example of a Big Brain moment that saved the day for a tired and thirsty family.

Big Brain and Little Brain in Action: Amusement Park—Not So Amusing

It is a hot day at the amusement park, and a weary father brings his three small children into one of the indoor eating areas after a long day. He wants to get some water for his children. No one is at the front desk and there is no one waiting, so he walks to an empty table. Shortly after the family sits down, a host walks to their table and says, "You are supposed to wait to be seated" and points to a sign. The father frowns and exclaims, "I just need to get some water right now." The host stalks away to talk to waiters at the beverage station and tell them about the rude man sitting in their station. Not one, not two, but *three* different servers take one look at this father and seem to assume the attitude that they don't want anything to do with him. He doesn't look happy. He looks exhausted, actually. And he looks a little angry. He and his children are tired and thirsty, really thirsty.

The father's mood does not improve when those three workers glance at him without saying anything and disappear into the back of the restaurant. "Doesn't anybody here want to help me?" the father asks plaintively.

A fourth waiter who is at a different station notices the father and his disappointment at the behavior of the other workers. She takes it upon herself to stop the cycle of Little Brain activity. Instead of walking away, she walks over to him. She smiles and asks in a kind tone, "What can I get you, sir?" Helping him is not her responsibility—he is not in her station—but she seizes the moment. She is responding from her Big Brain, and because of that, she shifts the father's whole way of thinking and acting from Little Brain to Big Brain.

"Right now I just need some water," the father says, his Little Brain soothed into a peaceful state by the warmth of the worker who has greeted him.

The worker nods, reaches into a nearby cooler, and hands the father two large bottles of water and some cups. As the frustrated father fumbles around for his money, the worker says, "No charge."

The father looks at her with surprise and smiles.

"Thank you," he says. "I really appreciate that."

The worker smiles back, and the father and his children begin to cool off in more ways than one.

That fourth waiter transforms what could have been a very unpleasant Little Brain situation into a nice, thirst-quenching Big Brain moment.

You don't always have to give people free stuff to make them happy. But, you do have to recognize the moment and respond. The more you identify Big Brain actions, the better you will get at creating your own. Like anything else—exercise will make it stronger.

CHAPTER TAKEAWAY

Life itself is a series of moments. Every new moment is like a new file opened on a computer. How will the other person in the moment label that file—in positive or negative terms? It's up to you. You get to decide the quality of the moments of your life when you take the initiative and come from your Big Brain.

Every Conversation Is
an Opportunity

One of the most important skills that a human being can possibly possess is the ability to have a great conversation. If you can have a great conversation, you can succeed at just about anything.

You can get your point across with ease, you can guide conversations to positive conclusions, and you can get the most from each encounter. You can also avoid problems with your friends and loved ones, and you can resolve them quickly and effectively if they do surface.

At work you can talk with your coworkers and even your boss and eliminate issues before they arise. You can create and maintain channels for clear communications.

One of the problems facing us today is that since many of us spend so much time staring into a computer screen instead of the face of another human being, we've all but lost the ability to have great conversations. So in this chapter, let's discuss the lost art of having great conversations because great communication is at the heart of every successful moment. We will also look at some places in a conversation where you can make a difference, places where you can take the conversation from Little Brain to Big Brain.

Continuing and New Conversations

Every day, you continue conversations with the people you've known for years. These conversations help you maintain your relationships with your spouse, children, siblings, parents, friends, coworkers, clients, and many others. They give you plenty of opportunities to change the direction of your relationships when necessary, clarify misunderstandings, and deal with problems in those relationships. They give you opportunities to make the relationships stronger.

You also begin new conversations with people you meet in the course of your day. You may feel that you will never see some of these people again, yet as time goes by, you realize that some of these seemingly unimportant conversations have turned into important, long-term relationships.

"Oh! What's That?"

One of the elements of a good conversation is to stay in the moment. This seems to be getting more difficult to do with every new invention. In some conversations, people will frequently look at their cell phones or other devices for their next message. Instead of listening to what is being said, they seem to be constantly saying "Oh, what's that?" This is the same as saying "Oh! I found something more interesting than what you are talking about" or "I hope someone more interesting is trying to contact me." This activity of constantly looking away will be one of the greatest challenges in our ability to manage and stay in the moment.

Whose Moment Is It, Anyway?

Another problem occurs all too often in conversations involving several people at once: someone in the group constantly tries to steer the conversation to his or her interest. At times, we all may be guilty of this. But sometimes you need to recognize that this conversation, this *moment*, is not about you!

You may need to facilitate the moment by not trying to make it relevant to yourself but instead allowing the conversation and the moment to be for others. Instead of cutting in or saying "Well, you know that same thing happened to me" and then stealing the conversation, you may find it beneficial to understand that not every moment is your moment. Sometimes the moment belongs to someone else.

Here's a story that shows how give-and-take facilitates that kind of conversation.

Big Brain and Little Brain in Action: The Story in the Conversation

Twice a year, Bob, Joan, Tom, and Danny, division managers for an insurance company, get together for dinner at the company conference to catch up.

On this night, Danny is the fastest talker and starts off with a story about his division's latest results. "They could be better, but we're holding our own," Danny explains. Bob follows with his own story about his career and how he is looking forward to a new position at national headquarters. "I can't wait to get out of my region." The conversation goes back and forth between Danny and Bob for some time. It's apparent that Joan wants to say something, but Danny and Bob are dominating the floor. Tom is quietly listening to everyone else, chiming in with an occasional comment.

The moment arrives when Danny and Bob finish their stories and pause. Tom takes advantage of the moment and looks at Joan. "Joan, tell us what's going on in your division. I noticed your numbers are up."

Joan says, "Thanks, Tom. Yes, we're experiencing a great quarter. We are fortunate to have a great group to work with, and they are really beginning to hit their stride."

Bob interrupts, "I wish mine would hit their stride. They are all underperforming. I may have to lay off some people."

"Really?" Tom says.

"Yeah, I got some people that are just not cutting it. Nothing I can do," Bob replies.

Danny says, "Hey, if they are not bringing in their numbers, it makes sense to get new people."

"That's really too bad. I don't like to lose people," Joan says.

Tom tries to steer the conversation back to Joan. "So, Joan, what is going on? Why do you think your numbers are up?"

Joan says, "Well, there are several reasons, but I would have to give the most credit to a new motivational method we stumbled upon when I was visiting a local office."

Danny exclaims, "We use those. I get my people tapes and books on how to stay focused. Once in a while I'll bring in a speaker to liven things up. I remember this one speaker who told the funniest jokes. He told this one about—"

Tom cuts Danny off. "Hold on, Danny. Joan, what is this thing you 'stumbled' upon?"

Danny says, "Sorry, Joan, go ahead."

"It's a little story that I promise will be worth the listen," Joan says. "I was covering for Steven, one of my branch managers, while he was on vacation. On the Friday before he left, he identified an agent sitting in the far corner and said, 'That's Cynthia. Don't expect much from her. We call that "grumpy corner." She transferred from another office several months ago. She is negative with everyone, so don't think it's because of anything you do. It's just the way she is. I'm thinking about getting rid of her when I get back. She does good work and her numbers are good, but the negative attitude just bothers people.'"

Bob's cell phone goes off. He looks at it and says, "Oh, it's nothing—just a reminder for tomorrow."

Everyone at the table stares at Bob. He says, "Oops! My apologies."

"I can't wait to hear how a bad apple helped you find a method to motivate people. I'm all ears," Danny says somewhat sarcastically.

Joan continues, "I thought that if I was going to be there for a week, I would take the opportunity see if I could work on grumpy corner. On Monday I made it a point to say hello to everyone—especially to Cynthia as she walked by my office."

"And?" Tom prompts.

"Cynthia looked at me and said nothing and went to her desk. At the end of the day she grabbed her stuff and was gone before I could try to engage her in a conversation.

"On Tuesday I did the same thing with the same results. I even made two attempts during the day to engage her in conversation, but nothing."

"Sometimes there is nothing you can do," Bob says.

"On Wednesday she called in sick."

"I have some like that—always taking time off," Bob acknowledges.

"Cynthia was not there, so I went to her desk and looked at the walls. This was one of the most organized places I have ever seen. It was complete with charts and graphs on the wall and a calendar that projected out three months with an action plan for each week."

"Wow," Tom says.

Joan continues, "I had called a staff meeting for Wednesday to discuss the office's performance. As the meeting began, one of Cynthia's coworkers said, 'Well, at least Grumpy's not here.' Several others chimed in with their agreement. Then it came to me: I had to change their attitude toward Cynthia if I was going to get her to change her attitude.

"I stopped the meeting. 'I want to show you something,' I said to them. I led them to her desk, showed them how efficiently she had organized her space, and let them know how impressed I was. They were all surprised, as none of them had ever ventured over there. 'Look at how much pride she has in her space.'

"The next day as Cynthia walked by my office, she stopped and said, 'Good morning, Mrs. Collins.' Then she continued to her desk.

"At the end of the day I heard a knock on my door. Cynthia walked in with her coat and bag in her hands. 'I just wanted to say thank you,' she began. 'I heard about what you said about me yesterday. It's the first nice thing anyone has said since I've been here.' She said good night and walked out."

Bob asks, "So what's the stumble?"

"Until that moment," Joan says, "I don't think I realized that even if people are not there, they will hear what you are saying about them. And more important, if you are saying nice things behind their backs, you can motivate people even when they are not present."

"Do you have a name for this stumble?" Tom asks.

Joan says, "Yes, we call it *good gossip*. It works similar to bad gossip, but it has a much more positive effect. We use it division-wide. Now all of our branch managers take advantage of the times when someone is not present to highlight that person's achievements. It seems to mean more to people than an award or a plaque on the wall."

Danny says, "Good gossip, hmmm?"

Tom looks at Bob. "Bob, what is that blank stare?"

Bob replies, "I was just thinking that if they hear the nice things when they are not there, they must also hear the bad things even when they are not there."

Joan says, "That, gentlemen, was our greatest lesson of all: everyone hears everything."

Whether you use your Big Brain or your Little Brain has more relevance today than at any time in the past. At no other time in history have we had so many ways to connect with people, so many devices to communicate through, and so many chances to express ourselves. But are all those devices really helping us to communicate?

CHAPTER TAKEAWAY

Every conversation has opportunities to create memorable moments. Just by being present and attentive in the conversation, you'll more likely be able to recognize whose moment it is—and be able to make the most of it for everyone. And remember, good gossip creates a powerful legacy.

The Paradox of Communication Tools

Today, we live in an era of unprecedented communication tools. We have e-mail, instant messaging, Twitter, Facebook, texting, chat, video chat, and who knows what's next. And as a bonus, each one of our comments is recorded on a digital device somewhere for the whole world to see or hear—if not now, at some point in the future. We also have the ability to stay in touch *forever* with everyone who knows us, and the people we know have the ability to stay in touch with us *forever*.

Communicating in today's technology-rich world allows for so many more opportunities to send messages, so many more opportunities to use the Big Brain or the Little Brain. It allows us to broadcast our thoughts to everyone. It also allows us to make mistakes faster, put those mistakes on many different devices, and send them to more people than we ever thought possible.

Technology can be an enabler for the Little Brain. The Little Brain just loves to send those nasty e-mails, text messages, and updates, regardless of the consequences down the road.

As recent global events show, used properly technology is beneficial. It can quickly get out needed information, it can be used as a follow-up communication tool, and it can answer important questions, from homework to simply "Where are you?" It can also be a handy tool for keeping parents connected to their children and a great way for friends to stay in touch over time.

Communication Tools— or Miscommunication Tools?

Unfortunately, few of these communication tools allow individuals to look directly into each other's eyes. Instead, we stare at a screen or talk on the phone while we are doing something else. This electronic world disconnects us from the human emotional cues we use to understand people. This makes it difficult to fully appreciate the other person's tone and body language, as well as other key components of good communication.

In business and in our private lives, if we aren't communicating consciously in a conversation, we risk searching for a quick retort. In doing so we often end up activating our Little Brain instead of our Big Brain. We say the first words that come into our heads, which, unfortunately, can be very inconsiderate, self-centered, or even hurtful. This may set off a cycle of Little Brain communication.

When we feel hurt or injured by a Little Brain comment, our reaction can easily come from our Little Brain. We can lash out and say something even more hurtful. This is how the cycle escalates with each exchange.

We see it all too often. Many people fail at relationships because of poor communication skills. This can lead to unhappy homes, frustrating workplaces, and aggravating lives.

When we operate from our Little Brain, we fail to recognize what the moment requires. Relationships often fail because we get trapped in Little Brain wars, trying to win arguments at any cost.

Digital devices don't seem to be helping matters. In fact, misunderstandings and miscommunications can happen more often because we are trying to interpret the pixels in front of us instead of the people in front of us. Although they can facilitate exchanging information fast, our devices are not the best tools for real communication.

Big Ears, Little Ears

One byproduct of all these technological advances is that we are beginning to use our ears less and less. We are missing the tone of the message as the text appears in front of us.

When we do use our ears, the Big Brain and the Little Brain are right there, challenging each other for control of the message. The Big Brain wants to hear everything that is being said to completely understand the communication. The Little Brain filters the message to eliminate anything it doesn't want to hear.

The Big Brain truly listens to what the other person is saying. It gives that person the attention deserved because it wants to be engaged in the conversation. The Big Brain is a master of the art of listening.

Instead of the art of listening, on the other hand, the Little Brain practices the art of lying in wait. While the other person is talking, the Little Brain is waiting for an opening so it can continue with what it wants to say. It has little regard for the conversation.

To illustrate the impact the digital age is having on all communication, let's look at these exchanges between an intern and the vice president of a public relations company.

Big Brain and Little Brain in Action:
Texting It In

Ryan, fresh out of college, is in his final week of interning for a public relations company. He is looking for a way to turn the last three months of hard work without pay into hard work *with* pay. He has worked a lot for the vice president of marketing, Greg Fenton. Greg is out of town the next two weeks, and Ryan realizes he will not see him again by the time he leaves. He is so eager to speak to Greg that instead of waiting to set up an appointment, he sends Greg a text, asking if he knows of any positions opening up:

> Hi Mr. Fenton,
>
> As you know my time is coming to an end. I was wondering if you know of any positions opening up soon. I truly appreciate any advice you can forward to me.
>
> Thank you,
> Ryan Johnston

Here's Greg's response:

> sorry, nothing I know of.
> G

That's it—the whole reply.

Ryan writes back, this time shortening his message based on Greg's text.

> Mr. Fenton,
>
> I realize there may be nothing now, but could you please keep me in mind if something does come up?
>
> Thanks,
> Ryan

Here's Greg's final reply:

> doubt it—no money
> G

Greg's message may have been the truth, but it was so short that it leaves a lot to interpretation. Ryan's Little Brain translates the reply as "We got what we needed from you, so don't bother me."

The abbreviated texting world is making its way into all communications at all levels, and we are losing a bit of our language in the process. Greg's e-mails do not even start with a capital letter. They were likely sent from a cell phone. The convenience of sending a message from a cell phone has led to the rationalization that the rules of English no longer apply.

Person to Person

If Ryan had waited for Greg to return and then requested a meeting, the exchange would have gone much differently. No doubt Greg's response would have been far more professional. Perhaps the opportunity to hear the tone of the words would have added dimension to the exchange. The moment might even have been peppered with some suggestions and recommendations.

All Is Not Lost

Ryan's Big Brain does take Greg's short uninformative texts as a setback, but Ryan does not take it personally. He decides he will look somewhere else in the company.

He resets his sights on the graphics department and sends an e-mail to the head of the division, Jane Andrews.

> Good morning, Ms. Andrews.
>
> My name is Ryan Johnston. I have been an intern over the summer and my time here is drawing to a close. I really like this company and am looking forward to applying for some positions as they become available. When you have time, would it be possible for me to meet with you and get some advice on how to proceed?
>
> Thank you,
> Ryan Johnston

Here's Jane's response:

> Hi, Ryan,
>
> Sure. I would love to meet with you to see if I can be of any assistance. You know this is a great company, and even if

there is nothing right now, I am confident you will be able to apply for something very soon.

Please call my secretary, Marsha, at extension 2344 to set up a time when we can speak.

Sincerely,
Jane Andrews
VP Graphics

A better response, a brighter outlook—changing the approach and the medium (from text to e-mail) can change the results.

Moments in Time

So far, we've looked at moments that involve mostly you and one other person. But what happens when you're talking to a few people—or even many people—at the same time? How do you stay in Big Brain mode under those challenging circumstances?

CHAPTER TAKEAWAY

Today's technology has made it easier to give people your thoughts instantly, but having the ability to do something does not always mean that it needs to be done. Sometimes you may want to take some time before you communicate. Once you push Send or Reply All, your message belongs to someone else.

Managing Multiple Moments—
the Social Media Effect

At times you will be managing multiple moments—or at least trying to manage them.

In this era of exploding social media, smart phones, and other devices, many of the conversations we have never really end! In addition, they are developing at an increased velocity that leaves us less and less time to formulate a response. Often, this *speed communicating* results in reactions and messages you would like to take back. But once you push Send, that is the end of your ability to edit your comments. In addition to speed, the sheer number of conversations you have going on at one time has increased dramatically. Managing these multiple conversations—and the multiple moments and their legacies—requires you to develop an entirely new set of communication skills to keep the Big Brain in control of the messages.

Having a heart-to-heart, eye-to-eye communication seems to be a dying art. It is being replaced with digital messages coming at us from all directions. And yet even our digital communiqués seem to be deteriorating at a rapid pace. They have gone from fully spelled-out messages to short blurts of information, as we saw in the previous chapter.

We have (or at least we think we have) become good at carrying on multiple "conversations" at the same time. We believe we can chat with a few friends online, check a Facebook page, and talk on the phone, all while trying to read something.

However, this type of multitasking compromises our communication with everyone. Although we are exchanging information with a number of people, can we say that we are truly listening? Are we really engaged and paying attention? What are we missing? These moments create perfect opportunities for Little Brain comments to creep in.

Your reactions to others and the influences in your life that affect those reactions take on more significant roles as the ability to instantaneously communicate proliferates.

Digital communication via a beeper was once an occasional interruption in our lives. Today's devices have become, for many, a valued communication necessity. For others, they have crossed the line to become an obsession.

Texting While Driving— an Unmanageable Combination

Driving is already a multitasking event. You have to watch where you are going, constantly check what the cars around you are doing, and look out for unexpected dangers—and now you have to look out for people who are texting or talking on their cell phones while driving. Add your own texting to such an important responsibility, and you can see why driving and texting is not only illegal but totally irresponsible.

Texting while driving is as Little Brain as you can get.

When you're driving, you are maneuvering a two thousand–pound pile of metal and fiberglass on wheels at thirty to fifty miles an hour while passing cars two feet away from you coming in the opposite direction at thirty to fifty miles an hour. During this powerful exchange of faith that other drivers are paying attention, what do you do when you get a text or hear your phone ring? The idea that you have to answer it "now" is like letting the Little Brain take total control of the vehicle. Think about what the Little Brain does to a simple conversation and imagine it in control of a car.

If you get a text while driving, let the Big Brain keep control of the car. If you really need to see who is texting or calling you, pull over and deal with it.

One Degree of Separation

Although not as dangerous as texting while driving, texting our way through our social media lives has its own risk. Before social networking, the past mostly stayed in the past. You may have even had some level of privacy. Now, because of the permanence of your digital diaries, visible for all your "friends" to see, your past can live on someone else's computer forever and your privacy is beginning to evaporate. (The true length of "forever" can't yet be calculated, but it's going to be an awfully long time.)

Since any information, any pictures, and any comment posted on a social network site or sent via cell phone or e-mail could go global instantly, it's essential to develop the communication skills that allow you to successfully have multiple moments going on simultaneously and still create Big Brain legacies. The story of Lisa and George shows how this can play out.

Big Brain and Little Brain in Action: The Past Is Present

Lisa is finishing a conversation with her ex-boyfriend George on her hands-free cell phone as she pulls her car into the parking lot at work. "Look," she says, "I don't want to talk about this anymore. I want to move on. We broke up for a lot of reasons. I need you to lose my number!" She hangs up the phone frustrated and realizes that her last comment was probably a little too harsh, but says to herself, "I'll deal with it tonight."

As she parks, she gets a text from a friend inviting her to party tonight. She returns the text as she is walking to her position at the reception desk at a small hotel.

After she settles in behind the front desk, her phone buzzes again, but she cannot answer it. She waits until no one is watching and then sneaks the phone out from her pocket. It is a text from her friend Maggie telling her she must check her Facebook page immediately: "George has posted photos, and they are not flattering."

Lisa is concerned but can't get to a computer until her break. On her break, she uses one of the computers at work to check her Facebook status. When her page comes up, she sees photographs of last year's trip to the Caribbean with George. The pictures show her scantily clad and completely drunk. She lets out a loud profanity. A coworker from another room walks up behind her and exclaims, "Wow! Did not know you were such a party animal." Lisa's manager walks in and says, "Did I hear foul language? That's not allowed. What if a guest heard you?" Lisa says nothing.

Lisa shuts off the screen before the manager sees what was on it, but does not turn off the computer.

Back at the front desk, she keeps making mistakes and must repeat several entries for guests checking in. She's distracted because she knows her mother is on her Facebook page, and she is wondering how to get those photos off before anyone sees them.

At lunch, Lisa is in damage-control mode. She calls, texts, e-mails, and pokes her ex-boyfriend to see if she can reach him.

The afternoon seems quiet but as Lisa walks to the back room for her break, she sees her Facebook page up on the computer with several coworkers looking at it.

"Damn!" she says.

"Hey, you left it up," a coworker says.

"But that's private!"

"It was until you opened it here."

That evening as she walks to her car, a different coworker makes a crude gesture referring to the photos. Lisa sits in her car talking to a friend on her cell when she gets a text from another friend who saw the photos.

Driving home that night, Lisa is talking on her cell phone when she gets a text. She is desperate to see if it is her ex. She glances over at her phone and the car begins to drift, almost hitting another car. Exasperated, she pulls over and stops the engine. The text is from George: "Took the pictures down . . . for now."

At home that night, Lisa's mom calls her aside and tells her that not only did she see the photos but it was a neighbor who told her about them.

Lisa spends the most of the night making adjustments to her social media sites. She calls George and apologizes for the "lose my number" comment. George does the same for posting the photos. He agrees to never put them up again.

Lisa looks at her cell phone. She now has over two dozen unread texts from friends—all about the photos.

Here to Stay

Much like automobiles revolutionized the way the world commuted at the turn of the last century, smart phones and similar devices have begun to revolutionize the way we communicate.

The automobile was not welcomed by everybody when it first arrived on the scene, but the automobile did not go away. Technology is also here to stay. It is getting smaller, cheaper, faster, and more accessible, seemingly every hour. It will be up to us to decide whether it becomes an asset to the way we live or an interruption to the way we communicate.

So whether you are dealing with a one-on-one situation or you are managing multiple moments with a wide variety of people on several different devices, you've got to be on top of your game in every moment. The moment that gets away will come back to haunt you. Can you manage multiple moments? Of course you can—as long as you keep your Big Brain ahead of your Little Brain.

CHAPTER TAKEAWAY

Managing multiple moments can be very challenging, but that's what we think we have to do in today's multiplatform, multitasking, hyperspeed world. The danger is not only poor communication but also living a distracted life. As technology becomes a greater part of your life, your past will always be present, and your privacy will slip away.

Attack of the Little Brain—
What You Can Do

What happens if you have every intention of creating a positive moment, but the other person is coming at you with his or her Little Brain firmly activated? Before you even have a chance to open your mouth, the other person is attacking you, criticizing you, or otherwise entering the encounter in a decidedly Little Brain, negative way.

Your natural tendency, when you are attacked in a Little Brain manner, is to counterattack with your Little Brain. It's the old fight-or-flight response. The Little Brain loves fight or flight. If you *fight*, if you react in an equally angry or inappropriate manner, the Little Brain wins—but you lose. If you choose *flight*, if you leave the situation either by stomping away from the person or by withdrawing emotionally or shutting down, it's another victory for the Little Brain. But it's another loss for you and the people around you. The challenge is to find a way to respond effectively, from your Big Brain, even in the face of an attack from the other person's Little Brain.

It isn't easy.

So how do you begin to respond from your Big Brain when you're being attacked by someone else's Little Brain? First, *don't take it personally*.

Recognize that when people are coming from their Little Brains, they are often *under the influence* of something else in their lives (remember the enchilada story) and the attack is not personal to you, even if it seems like it is, even if they say it is.

It all comes down to being conscious of what you are trying to accomplish right now, in this moment. You want to have as many positive moments with other people as you possibly can. Your goal—to respond from your Big Brain—doesn't change even though other people are reacting from their Little Brains. In fact, at times like these your Big Brain needs to work at double speed.

So what exactly do you do in the moment?

Don't Win the Argument—Win the Moment

Start by taking a deep breath. Take three deeps breaths. You don't have to respond immediately. Regroup! Invite your Little Brain to sit out this confrontation, and invite your Big Brain to take over.

Allow your Big Brain to drive the moment. When you are confronted with a Little Brain attack, don't try to win the argument by responding with your Little Brain. That will only escalate the encounter into a Little-Brain-to-Little-Brain frenzy, where no one wins. Allow your Big Brain to take over and to find the right way to give the moment a positive ending. After the moment has passed, those involved will recognize what you did. They will recognize your patience and ability to not get sucked into a Little Brain argument, and with that you create a positive legacy and win the moment.

What's Influencing This Moment?

When you're attacked by someone in Little Brain mode, it's a good time to *review the influences* we discussed previously. What is influencing him to act like that? What is it about her that's activating her Little Brain? If you can stop and think about those questions, just for a second, your highly emotional and impulsive Little Brain will automatically begin to calm down. Your more rational Big Brain will begin to kick in.

Even if no particular influences come to mind, you can still take control of the situation. Remind yourself that you might have an angry person in front of you, but your task is to *take control of the moment*. Even though the conversation may not be starting out in a friendly way, you still want to create the best possible outcome.

Change Your Attitude—Change the Outcome

At any point in an encounter, you have the opportunity to change your attitude by switching your tone or using different words or just becoming more aware of the influences in the moment. When you change your attitude, you will change the outcome—and the legacy.

Here's an example of how someone can change from Little Brain to Big Brain thinking while still in the moment.

Big Brain and Little Brain in Action: Late Arrival

Fred has been doing a good job at work, but this morning, he arrives very late. His boss meets him at the front door. "You're late," says Ms. Stone, his manager.

"Genius!" Fred says in a snide tone of voice as he begins to walk by her. "I guess that's why they made you the manager!"

Ms. Stone can't believe her ears. Fred's Little Brain reaction awakens her Little Brain from its slumber.

"What did you say?" she asks angrily, on the verge of disciplining Fred then and there.

Suddenly Fred wakes up! He becomes aware that his Little Brain began the encounter, and his awareness helps him shift on the spot from Little Brain to Big Brain mode.

"I'm sorry, Ms. Stone," he says. "I really am. I got into a small car accident on my way to work—someone hit me. When the police asked for my insurance, I didn't have it with me. And now I have to go to court to show proof "

A Big Brain change of attitude turns away Ms. Stone's potential wrath.

"Fred," Ms. Stone says, much calmer, now that she's coming from *her* Big Brain, "thanks for letting me know. When do you have to appear?"

"Next Monday at 9:00 a.m.," Fred says. "That'll make me late again."

"No worries, Fred," Ms. Stone says. "It could happen to anyone. We'll just expect you around noon on Monday."

So that's what it looks like when you go from Little Brain to Big Brain mode. And it's a good thing Fred did. Otherwise, he might be reading the want ads on Monday while he waits to show proof that he has insurance.

CHAPTER TAKEAWAY

Little Brain moments are a part of life. When you find yourself being confronted with other people's Little Brains, take a step back and see if you can identify the influences that may be causing their reactions. Instead of trying to win the argument, work hard to win the moment and the legacy.

Big Brain and Little Brain— the Perpetual Race

In any conversation, in any moment, it's not as if either the Big Brain wins or the Little Brain wins and that's it. Instead, it is like a race that never ends. In truth, your Big Brain or your Little Brain can get activated or reactivated at any point in a conversation. Things can be going along really great, and all of a sudden your Little Brain gets activated and here it comes, ready to shoot your mouth off. So even though you begin an encounter or carry on a conversation with your Big Brain, you've got to remain on guard. That Little Brain is tricky—and it wants to jump in at any chance.

The key to keeping the Little Brain in its place is what we've been discussing all along—you must become aware of the influences that are acting on you and pay attention to your state of mind and the state of mind of the people with whom you are interacting. When you do, you have the opportunity to change your attitude, words, and tone of voice in a flash. In fact, you can at any point reset them for the rest of the encounter. You can snap out of Little Brain mode and guide your thinking toward a Big Brain legacy.

For example, let's say you find yourself in a gossipy conversation with two of your business associates who are making snide remarks about a third. You might be tempted to join in. That is when you'll experience a struggle between your Little Brain, which wants to add your own gossip to the mix and be seen as funny or informed, and your Big Brain, which wants you to get out of the conversation and stop perpetuating the gossip.

If you become aware of your Little Brain activity, you can use your Big Brain to direct the conversation away from the Little Brain. Or if the conversation doesn't seem to be something you can change, your Big Brain can direct you to stay silent or direct your feet to politely step away.

You always have a choice in any situation. Even if, in the above example, your Little Brain starts reacting by saying something inappropriate about the coworker, you can still change your focus from Little Brain to Big Brain and thus change the direction of your conversation, or at least your participation in it.

Snatching a Little Brain Legacy from a Big Brain Moment

Suppose you start your encounter in a Big Brain way, only to have the Little Brain sneak in a comment that you regret the moment you hear it leave your mouth. The following story shows how this type of situation can play out.

Big Brain and Little Brain in Action: A Discouraging Word

Mark is a salesperson working for a company that sells solar panels. The company just had its first positive quarter in over a year, and the upper management decides to bring in a motivational speaker named Jared to keep the momentum going.

Jared comes to a business meeting and gets everyone excited and motivated with great discussions about inspirational levels of sales and customer service. There's great back-and-forth with everyone participating—and it's all going forward on a Big Brain level. Mark and the other salespeople are really excited with the presentation.

Jared finishes by addressing Paul, the regional manager. "Paul, your team has done a great job of connecting with your clients, and it shows in your sales. It's been a pleasure for me to speak to all of you, and I hope you ask me to return."

A round of applause follows, and Mark excitedly exclaims, "Thank you! This has been one of the best meetings we have ever had!" Others vocalize their agreement.

Jared leaves the room, and everybody feels highly motivated to go out and sell like crazy.

Paul, in his eagerness to latch on to some of the accolades in the room and to remind people that he is still the boss, decides he wants to be the one to finish the meeting—he wants the last word. Before his Big Brain can stop him, he ends the meeting by saying "Well, remember, just because last month's numbers are good does not mean we can get lazy. I expect you all to work harder this month."

Suddenly, all of the positive energy drains out of the room. All that inspiration and motivation disappears, just because of one little comment—from the Little Brain of a big boss.

What was Paul thinking? He took what was a Big Brain inspirational moment and let his Little Brain turn it into a demotivating legacy. Unfortunately, Little Brain moments like this one show up all too often, and their legacies are far reaching.

CHAPTER TAKEAWAY

Each moment presents opportunities for you to choose how you will respond or react. The challenge is to keep your Big Brain in shape so it can beat the Little Brain every time. If your Big Brain is going to win the race, you have to stay in the moment.

Finishing the Encounter

As we said in chapter 3, a legacy is the positive or negative impressions we leave behind when an encounter has ended. Although legacies are left behind, they do not stay in the past. They later reappear in front of us at full strength, and they are not easy to elude.

The Big Brain will always look for ways to leave a moment on a positive note, even if disagreements remain. You can almost always find a way to work out problems if you are responding from your Big Brain.

The Little Brain, on the other hand, will be selfish and not care how the other person feels at the end of the exchange. The Little Brain will often end the moment using a negative tone or comment.

Here are some simple guidelines to help you finish your moments effectively.

Big Brain Finishing Touches

Here are some Big Brain finishing touches to increase the likelihood that your legacy will be positive:

- *Leave the moment in a positive way.* Make sure that the final comment from *you* is always positive.

- *Follow up with a thank-you.* Send a card or a note to recap the good time you had. Some stores like Nordstrom insist that their employees send thank-you notes to their customers. It's a great way to create a feeling of personal connection.
- *Clarify.* Send a well-worded note to clarify any possible misunderstandings that you might have had with the person. Often questions will come up long after the moment is over. Follow through and make sure the questions are answered. At night, doctors go over their charts to make sure that they didn't miss anything in their diagnoses. Likewise, the end of your day should be the time when you review your contacts with other people throughout the day—the moments you had—to make sure that you didn't miss anything.
- *Apologize.* If a moment has ended and you realize that you owe an apology for something you said or did or something you forgot to say or do, don't waste time. The faster the apology, the faster the healing.
- *Forgive.* If someone offers you an apology at the end of a moment, acknowledge the apology as soon as possible. However, be aware that every act of forgiveness needs processing time, and you may proceed at your own pace. Keep this in mind when you're apologizing to others as well. Don't assume that just because you've apologized they're ready to move on in their relationship with you just yet. Give them time.

Little Brain Brush-offs

Here is a look at some Little Brain brush-offs that bring about Little Brain legacies:

- *Leave the moment in a negative way.* You purposely end the moment negatively as a way of getting even or getting back at someone. The price for such behavior is steep—it can cost you relationships and much more.

- *Do not follow up.* You fail to follow through on what you agreed to do during the moment.
- *Fail to clarify misunderstandings.* You know that the other person may have gotten the wrong impression from you or remember a detail that would help to clarify perceptions, yet you fail to act on this knowledge.
- *Refuse to apologize.* You realize that you may have made a mistake, and you know a simple apology would be helpful, but your ego and pride keep you from taking the time to apologize.
- *Do not not forgive.* You receive an apology from someone and do not allow forgiveness to occur. Remember, you don't have to forgive the person that second. But if you bear a grudge, your Little Brain baggage will only get heavier.

CHAPTER TAKEAWAY

Your choice as to how you finish an encounter will have an impact on the legacy of the moment. Take the time to review your recent encounters and see if any items were left unresolved and need follow-up.

What Legacies Are You Creating?

W e've seen that every encounter with another human being opens a moment, an opportunity for you to create, improve, worsen, or even destroy a relationship, whether that relationship is longstanding or brand new. Not all moments will rise to the point of creating significant legacies. But the moments that do will create legacies that can be deeply beneficial or deeply wounding.

To assist you in remembering the key concepts in this book and explaining them to others, we have used some simple images: the Big Brain legacy deposit and the Little Brain baggage.

The Big Brain Legacy

The essence of the Big Brain legacy is an increase in trust. After an encounter with you, the other person leaves thinking "You're a person I can trust" or "I like you." That's true whether the other person in the conversation is your customer, coworker, spouse, significant other, parent, or child.

No matter who the other person is, the Big Brain legacy is always added *trust*. And when the legacy is positive, the person with whom you had the encounter will place a deposit into your Big Brain Legacy Bank and Trust (fig. 15.1).

You'll have a different Big Brain legacy bank account with every person you encounter in your life.

Figure 15.1 The Big Brain Legacy Bank and Trust

The Little Brain Legacy

The primary Little Brain legacy is a decrease in trust. After an encounter with you, the other person thinks "I don't think you were telling the truth" or "I'm not sure I can trust you." That's the last thing you want anybody to think about you! That thought goes into the Little Brain baggage you will carry with that person (fig. 15.2). The Little Brain baggage you carry whenever you deal with that person only gets heavier every time a Little Brain legacy is attached to a moment you created.

Figure 15.2 Little Brain baggage

You'll have different Little Brain legacy baggage with every person you encounter in your life.

How to Lighten Your Baggage

Little Brain legacies are permanent unless you take steps to remove them from your baggage. You can do this by identifying where you have left Little Brain legacies with particular people and seeking ways to undo them. You may need to offer an apology that's long overdue, fulfill a forgotten promise, or do something as simple as make a phone call or initiate some other communication for which the person has been waiting.

When you carefully look back, you will be able to identify the baggage that you are carrying around, which will allow you to do something about it.

CHAPTER TAKEAWAY

The legacies of each moment will come back to you in the form of baggage you will have to carry or deposits you get to bank. They will increase the level of trust people have in you, or they will diminish the trust people have in you. Be conscious and aware of the moments with others that make up your day, and strive to create positive legacies.

PART THREE

Recognizing the Opportunities in the Moment

By now, you're probably pretty good at spotting Big Brain responses and Little Brain reactions, and you may even have started to practice taking your time and making sure you are in control of the moments of your day.

Now we will look at some tools that will help you keep your Big Brain in control and identify the traps we all fall into once in a while. Once you're aware of these tools and traps, your communication skills will be stronger.

Going forward, your responsibility is to make as many moments of your day positive, Big Brain experiences for you and for all involved.

How do you do that every single time? By taking advantage of the opportunities every moment presents.

Every moment offers different opportunities. However, when you're right in the middle of a moment, it's sometimes a challenge to notice your opportunities for using your Big Brain versus your Little Brain.

In this part, you will learn how to identify seven different *opportunities in the moment* within the encounters of your life. These are the opportunities that most commonly arise when people engage with each other. For each opportunity, you can use a Big Brain tool to make the moment end positively and create a deposit for your

Big Brain Legacy Bank and Trust, or you can fall into a Little Brain trap that twists the moment into negativity, which adds to your legacy baggage.

As with any trap, if you see it ahead of time, you've got a better chance of avoiding it. And the good news is that learning how to recognize the traps is a skill that you'll get better at with every moment. The more traps you recognize, the more opportunities you'll have to avoid them. Every trap can be substituted with a tool and, unfortunately, vice versa.

Here are the seven *opportunities* for picking up a tool or falling into a trap:

- Awareness
- Tone
- Words
- Control
- Time
- Responsibility
- Power

We'll go through them one by one and learn about the legacies for both Big Brain responses and Little Brain reactions.

Awareness

Yogi Berra used to joke, "You can observe a lot just by watching." Awareness isn't some kind of unattainable state of mind—it's just the practice of watching closely. When you're aware of what's going on in a given moment, you have the insight to choose rather than follow. Without awareness, you run the risk of blindly following others or carelessly following your impulses, even when these are leading you astray.

Finally, awareness keeps you from being distracted by the chatter of the superficial influences around you. It gives you the vision to see the moment for what it is and what it can potentially become.

Awareness reminds us that at any time in any moment, we have the power to change the direction of the exchange and the legacy of the moment.

Strengthening your awareness provides you with three tools. Floating through life unaware puts you at risk of falling into three traps. Let's look at these traps and tools.

Awareness Tool

What if you started moments by telling yourself, "I want some good to come out of this encounter; I want to be careful what I say"? You would be using the tool of awareness.

As a result, you would

- Recognize the influences you are under *and* the influences others are under before you respond.
- Know who is in the room when you are speaking—and whom they might talk to about what is said.
- Keep the legacy of the moment in mind.

What's the legacy of awareness? People will think you are sharp. Sharpness becomes a positive part of your reputation, a deposit in the Big Brain Bank and Trust.

Unawareness Trap

When you fall into the trap of unawareness, you wander into moments telling yourself, "It's not like the whole world can hear what I am saying." As a result, you

- Fail to recognize the influences you are under in the moment.
- Pay no attention to the influences that might be affecting others.
- Are oblivious to who might be in the room and speak without regard for whom you might offend.

What's the legacy of unawareness? People will think you are clueless. Their memory of your cluelessness is Little Brain baggage you will have to carry around with you.

Not Taking It Personally Tool

When you use the tool of not taking it personally, you understand that "This is not about me." As a result, you

- Know that even when someone directs a harsh, personal-sounding jab at you, that person is probably under the influence of something else in his or her life.
- See beyond the moment.
- Give others time to get perspective and come to their senses.

What's the legacy of not taking it personally? You will be respected. You can deposit that respect in the Big Brain Bank and Trust.

Taking It Personally Trap

When you fall into the trap of taking it personally, you believe that others are attacking you. As a result, you

- Think everything others do and say is a personal attack.
- Focus on self-pity, telling yourself, "This always happens to me."
- Feel like the world is against you.

What's the legacy of taking it personally? People will think you are immature. Their memory of your immaturity is Little Brain baggage that you will have to carry with you.

Anticipating Tool

When you begin moments by saying "I've been thinking about this" instead of "I know what is going to happen" you are using the tool of anticipating. With this tool you

- Prescript the positive rather than the negative.
- Plan the desired legacy before the encounter begins—and keep focused on it.

- Anticipate potential traps that could arise during the encounter and eliminate them by addressing them up-front.

What's the legacy of anticipating? People will think you are really organized. Their memory of your organization skills becomes a good part of your reputation that you can deposit in the Big Brain Bank and Trust.

Assuming the Negative Trap

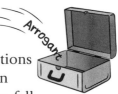

Assuming something negative brings negative emotions to the moment, which are difficult to get rid of even when the assumptions are proved wrong. When you fall into the trap of assuming the negative, you

- Prescript a negative outcome and play out the encounter before it occurs.
- Engage in self-imposed ignorance by wanting only enough information to validate your feelings and beliefs—and to prove that your script was right.
- Refuse to hear all sides because it might make you uncomfortable. (After all, how could you be wrong?)
- Gather only bits of information and fill in the rest with desired assumptions.

What's the legacy of assuming the negative? People will think you are arrogant. Arrogance is a trait that you will have to carry in your Little Brain baggage.

In every moment of customer relations, staying aware of what the customer wants is the key to a successful encounter. Even when things initially go wrong, it is still possible to save the encounter.

Awareness Tools and Traps in Action: Counter Encounters

Bruce, a human resource director at a large company, has had a long and stressful morning at work. He's on his lunch break, waiting to order at the counter of one of his favorite restaurants. When it's finally his turn, he's wrapped up in thoughts about work pressures and is *unaware* of what's happening in the present moment. He orders a Cajun Chicken Sandwich—when what he really wanted was a Cajun Chicken Salad.

When his order comes out, he's very hungry—and very disappointed not to have gotten what he wanted. He goes back to the counter and tells the cashier, "I believe I ordered a Cajun Chicken Salad." Because he's focused on his influences of hunger and stress, his tone is filled with anxiety. He is sure he ordered correctly and that the mistake is the cashier's.

Big Brain Response

When Bruce arrives at the counter with his complaint about receiving a sandwich instead of a salad, the cashier remembers that he specifically ordered the sandwich, but she does not challenge Bruce. Instead she tells him, "No problem. Let me get that to you right away. I apologize for the mistake."

"Okay," Bruce says. "Thank you."

He returns to his table and in a few minutes, his food arrives. While he's finishing his lunch—and relaxing away from the influences of hunger and stress—he thinks back to the way he ordered and suddenly remembers that he spoke incorrectly.

On his way out, he approaches the cashier again. "I think I actually ordered it wrong," he tells the cashier. "My mistake."

"No worries," the cashier says with a smile. "As long as you got what you wanted, we're happy. See you soon."

The legacy? That night when Bruce joins his friends for dinner, he tells everyone the story and gives the restaurant a very warm recommendation. The cashier understood that customers may not always be right, but in the moment they believe they are right, and that is all that matters. She knew what legacy she wanted from the moment. She wanted the customer to return in the future.

Little Brain Reaction

But what if the cashier had chosen a trap rather than a tool? What if she had taken personally the inference that she was wrong? What if it went like this:

The cashier sighs. She doesn't take time to become aware of what might be influencing Bruce's anxiety. "Let me see your receipt," she says. Bruce hands it to cashier. She looks at it and then she points at it. "No, look," she tells Bruce. "It says right here, 'Sandwich!'" Her tone says, "I told you so."

Now Bruce is completely fed up, and his Little Brain kicks in. "I know what it says," he snaps. "But that is not what I ordered."

"Are you saying I made a mistake?" the cashier snaps back—now fully in Little Brain mode herself.

"No," Bruce says with a tone of annoyance. He is feeling backed into a corner and says, "I just want what I want, and you screwed up my order."

But the cashier's pride is now involved and she doesn't want to back down. "I have to call my manager."

"Just give me my money back," Bruce demands.

"Fine."

Bruce gets his money and storms out. The rest of the afternoon he is under the negative influence of what happened at lunch. Later that evening, he meets several friends for dinner, and he tells the whole table about his lunch order, how amazed he was that he had to get into an argument just to try to get lunch—and how he is never going back.

The legacy? That restaurant loses Bruce *and his friends* as customers. And if Bruce goes online to record his dissatisfaction with the service, he could influence hundreds of others to eat elsewhere. Who knows how much lost business Bruce represents?

CHAPTER TAKEAWAY

Awareness is an important tool you can use to recognize what is happening in the moment. It can also help you anticipate and avoid taking things personally. Being aware of who is in the room and whom they will talk to allows you to keep your comments and their legacies in perspective.

Tone

In the story in the previous chapter, awareness is a driving factor in creating a positive or negative legacy for Bruce and the restaurant. But another area of opportunity that plays a large role in determining the outcome of the exchange between the cashier and Bruce is tone.

As infants, we begin learning to communicate with our parents or caretakers by using tone. Long before we understand a single word, it's the tone of the people leaning over our cradles and smiling, cooing, and laughing that helps us know what they are saying. Babies can tell if their parents or caretakers are happy or sad—or frightened because they are in danger. They quickly learn to respond to these tone cues and stay safe and happy.

As we grow, we begin connecting words with tones, but even as our vocabularies expand, we never lose our ability to read a tone by itself. We can even tell when the same words spoken in different tones mean something entirely different. Throughout our lives, tone continues to be far more important than words themselves in getting messages across. The tone is the message.

We hear a message's tone even before our brains have time to process the meaning of the words involved. Just as we see and understand people's facial expressions before understanding their words, a tone can be an audio smile—or an audio frown. It's the audible signal of a person's mood, and there are as many different tones as there are emotions. So identifying the particular tone being used is crucial to going beyond mere vocabulary and really getting clarity about what a person is saying.

Tone is one of the strongest indications you'll get about whether a person—and that person can be you yourself—is coming from the Big Brain or the Little Brain. Little Brain reactions and tones tend to escalate in both volume and intensity. Big Brain tones, on the other hand, are usually softer and calmer. They lay the foundation for a smooth exchange. A sustained soothing Big Brain tone can be a powerful inducement to others in the conversation to follow.

However, when we are frustrated, annoyed, uncomfortable, or just uneasy, the possibility of using our Little Brain tones increases. And if no one else in the exchange is coming from the Big Brain, those Little Brain tones will get louder and louder, and the temptation will be to match the latest tones or even one-up them. The negative tones will continue to escalate until an argument ensues, turning an encounter into a confrontation.

Little Brain tones, like air in a balloon, will expand and expand. They might start as annoyance or frustration and grow in negativity as the moment continues. Ultimately, the Little Brain

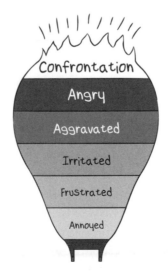

Figure 17.1 Little Brain tone balloon

tone balloon bursts—and that's never a positive ending. Figure 17.1 shows how tones can escalate until they explode.

Though Big Brain tones are less loud and showy than Little Brain tones, they can actually be more powerful. They have an undercurrent of strength, calm, and ease, and they can draw people to them, even in the presence of Little Brain tones. While Little Brain tones are a swelling balloon, Big Brain tones are a steady, solid foundation—a foundation for positive communication. Holding onto Big Brain tones even while others are using Little Brain tones is not only a sign of maturity but also of a strong Me. Figure 17.2 shows the foundation of Big Brain tones.

Figure 17.2 Big Brain tones

Let's look at some tools and traps related to tone.

Calmness Tool

Calmness is one of the most powerful tools. In its own way it has the ability to defuse tense situations and keep everyone focused. When you remain calm and use the tone that matches the desired results, you create clarity. You

- Read the tones of other people to gauge what influences they might be under.
- Recognize the tones of others and understand what they are truly communicating beneath their words.
- Bring others with you to an even tone.

What's the legacy of calmness? People will think you are comforting. You can deposit their feelings of comfort in the Big Brain Bank and Trust.

Escalation Trap

Escalation occurs when you confuse loudness with power. You think that the louder you are, the more power you have, and you are continually trying to one-up the tone or volume of others. When you reach the limits of loudness, your struggle to be the most powerful can quickly turn physical. But loudness is only the illusion of power. What it actually represents is weakness.

What's the legacy of escalation? You will seem angry. People will remember your anger, and you will have to carry a reputation as an angry person in your Little Brain baggage.

Positive Facial Expressions Tool

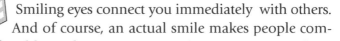

Smiling eyes connect you immediately with others. And of course, an actual smile makes people comfortable and expresses your intent to engage in a friendly exchange. Making sure your eyes, mouth, and facial expressions are in alignment is the first step to beginning a moment positively.

What's the legacy of positive facial expressions? People will think you are friendly. You can deposit a reputation for friendliness in the Big Brain Bank and Trust.

Negative Facial Expressions Trap

Physical cues are also a part of tone. Negative physical cues include rolling your eyes or having an annoyed or unconcerned expression. You might smirk or yawn, indicating to others that you just don't want to deal with the conversation. Even a shrug of the shoulders can show that you don't want to put forth the energy to be in the moment.

What's the legacy of negative facial expressions? People will remember that you were disrespectful. You will have to carry the reputation of disrespectfulness in your Little Brain baggage.

Hello and Good-Bye Tool

In written correspondence, your opening salutation is the textual smile that says hello in place of a welcoming facial expression and friendly tone. Writing "hello" and "good-bye" (or some version thereof) in *all forms* of digital text will open and close moments with a positive tone. When you leave a voice mail, be sure to use a positive tone that is clearly understood. Sometimes a nice tone at the end of a voice mail will be enough to make the listener smile.

What's the legacy of hello and good-bye? People will think you are pleasant to be around. You can deposit a reputation for pleasantness in the Big Brain Bank and Trust.

No Greeting, No Good-Bye Trap

Written words have a tone inferred by the reader, which means that written messages can be very tricky both to send and to read. The world of texting, tweets, and status updates has stripped away many opening salutations, and the practice is beginning to work its way into memos and even letters in the business world. We just rush straight to the message. But when you begin any written encounter without an opening salutation, it sets the tone of "I don't have time to be nice. Here is what I have to say, and you should read it." The readers are left to assume a tone—and often they may assume the wrong tone.

Likewise, when you close a message without saying some variation of good-bye, you're saying "*bad*-bye." You're ending abruptly, and the readers will be left feeling unclear or even insulted.

What's the legacy of no greeting, no good-bye? You will seem crude. You'll have to carry around a reputation for crudeness in your Little Brain baggage.

Tone is the message. In business or at home, the tones you use can convey the message more than the words you use. Everyone, no matter how old or young, understands the tone. As you will see in the story that follows, tone can mean the difference between an encounter that ends in anger and one that ends with a hug.

Tone Tools and Traps in Action:
"I Like That Tone Better, Daddy"

The power of a positive tone was one of the first lessons I learned in the journey that led me to creating *The Secrets of Successful Communication*. And the lesson came from my daughter when she was very little. As a matter of fact, I've learned a tremendous amount about communication from being the father of two wonderful kids, now teenagers. As in business, the close interactions of our family environments provide us with limitless opportunities to grow—or flounder.

I have to admit to making many communication mistakes early on when it came to parenting. I failed to pause and think when talking to my children. I quickly learned, however, that I had an amazing amount of power to make moments go well—and the same amount of power to make them go wrong—just by the way I handled the moment, just by the tone I used.

One Christmas Eve, I was under the tree stringing together lights when I saw the little feet of my daughter, Katelyn, only five at the time, start climbing up the ladder I'd set up to hang decorations. Obviously, she was not allowed to go up the ladder, and I immediately adopted my parental tone of concern with her. "Katelyn," I said sternly, "get down from there."

She paused for a second and then continued up the ladder. So I escalated my tone to grave concern. "Katelyn Rose. You get down."

She didn't respond. I was perplexed. Why wasn't she listening? This was unlike her.

I got out from under the tree, on the verge of getting angry. In my Little Brain, I was ready to escalate my tone to Parental DEFCON 1: "Did you hear me? I said get down!"

Big Brain Response

Before I could utter those unpleasant words—in an even more unpleasant tone—I noticed an angel in her hand that she was carrying toward the top of the tree. I looked at her and realized she was on the verge of tears.

In a much gentler tone, I said, "Honey, I need you to get down. It's dangerous."

Sniffling, she said, "I like that tone better, Daddy."

I was floored.

"But I wanted to put the angel on top," she whimpered.

Her desire to hang the angel was strong, and it meant a great deal to her. Until I understood that this was what was influencing her behavior, I could not respond properly. I was using the wrong tone.

"I'll put it up there for you," I told her.

"But I want to do it myself," she said in a very small voice.

Humbled, I answered, "Okay, honey. But I have to help you because it's not safe for you to go that high without me holding you."

"Okay, Daddy."

Later that night, Katelyn came into the living room with her pajamas on. She looked at the top of the tree. She ran over to me and gave me one of the most powerful hugs in the history of hugs.

"Thank you, Daddy. She is a very pretty angel, isn't she?"

I looked into my daughter's eyes. "Yes, she really is."

If my parental need to control that moment had won the argument, I would have lost one of the most precious memories of my life.

Little Brain Reaction

If my Little Brain tone had prevailed that night, the moment would have turned out very differently:

> Daddy: Did you hear me? I said get down!
> Katelyn: But I want to put the angel on the tree.
> Daddy: It's too dangerous. Now get down and give me the angel. I will put it on the tree.
> Katelyn: *(sniffling)* Okay.

Daddy puts the angel on the tree and Katelyn goes to her room crying. Later, when he goes to give her a kiss good night, instead of giving him a hug, she turns away under the covers.

CHAPTER TAKEAWAY

Tone is the message, and whether the communication is spoken words, facial expressions, text, or anything else, *it has a tone*. You always have the ability to set the tone of a moment and reset the tone throughout any encounter.

Words

The last chapter looked at how tone is one of the first components anyone you're speaking with will understand about your message, and so in many ways it gives others far more information than the actual words you choose. But of course, that doesn't mean you can just say anything. Your words are critical too—in fact, they're the third opportunity for creating a Big Brain moment.

When it comes to phrasing a message, the power is entirely in your hands. You get to choose the words that you're going to use. You get to choose exactly *when* you use them. And you get to choose *how* you use them.

Most people have a personal vocabulary of between 40,000 and 60,000 words, and we have access to the entire English language beyond that—over 750,000 words. That means the Big Brain and the Little Brain have access to all those words, too. Both brains are in a constant struggle to grab words and get them out faster than the other. But the Big Brain wants to think over those words and choose them carefully, while the Little Brain is comfortable just spitting something out.

Imagine the Big Brain and the Little Brain each have a spring-loaded compartment for quick access to words and phrases. They can fire them off as soon as the proper circumstances allow the spring to be released.

The Little Brain's storage compartment is stuffed with pent-up words and phrases that are building in pressure and desperately looking for their next chance to get out—whether that's at the right time or the wrong time. It's filled with every negative comeback, insult, snide remark, cliché, and inappropriate reaction you've ever contemplated. And the Little Brain is terrified of silence. It wants to release the spring and fill the silence with any one of those phrases, no matter what.

The Big Brain's storage compartment, by contrast, is filled with positive words and comments that reinforce the moment. And it is comfortable with something that the Little Brain isn't: silence. The Big Brain knows that sometimes silence and reflection can be an entirely appropriate response, especially when you need time to think matters through and consider your words.

But here's the catch. The Little Brain, as we know, is right next to the mouth. And this proximity gives the Little Brain's spring-loaded storage compartment a greater chance to get a comment out first. Ideally, the Big Brain would like to have some time to think about what to say. But because the Little Brain is always in a hurry, the Big Brain must have some quick, spring-loaded messages of its own, ready to go.

Now that we have a sense of the importance of words, and the power we have to choose which ones we use and how we use them, let's look at some word tools and traps.

Big Brain Spring-Loaded Response Tool

The Big Brain has to be constantly alert and work harder and faster to make sure that the Little Brain doesn't win the race to be the first to say something. The Little Brain is poised at the ready to fire off any bad joke, foolish reaction, or poorly crafted faux pas it can as fast as it can from its spring-loaded compartment. But with practice, the Big Brain can beat the Little Brain to the punch.

If you practice getting positive messages out faster than the Little Brain can fire negative ones, or simply allowing for silence

Figure 18.1 Examples of Big Brain spring-loaded responses

of thought before reacting, you're creating good moments and strengthening your Me. Figure 18.1 shows some examples of Big Brain spring-loaded response tools.

What's the legacy of a Big Brain spring-loaded response? You will seem clever. You can deposit a reputation for cleverness in the Big Brain Bank and Trust.

Little Brain Spring-Loaded Response Trap

Now that you know about the Little Brain's spring-loaded storage compartment, it's easy to see how it can be a trap. It includes hundreds of different negative words and responses and is loaded with many of the "oops" comments that

Figure 18.2 Examples of Little Brain spring-loaded reactions

you immediately regret the second they are uttered. You'll find some examples in figure 18.2. When you use sharp-witted but negative comments and harsh sarcasm to hurt or embarrass others, you may get a laugh, but ultimately, you lose the moment.

What's the legacy of a Little Brain spring-loaded reaction? People will think you are careless. You will carry a reputation for carelessness in your Little Brain baggage.

Good Words Tool

There's no reason why you can't use "replacement words" instead of profanity for intensity or as exclamations. If you take pause to realize that words can hurt, even those blurted on impulse, you'll begin to fill your Big Brain with more appropriate language. It may sound goofy to use words like "dang," "shucks," "or "dag nabbit," but when you think of the legacy words can create and how powerful words can be, you may find it worth your time to find replacement words for your Big Brain to use when your Little Brain wants to spit out foul language. Write down a list of all the bad words you use or have used. You will be surprised that you actually ever spoke them. Start eliminating them by making up your own replacement words for them.

What's the legacy of good words? You will seem thoughtful. Thoughtfulness is a good trait that you can deposit in the Big Brain Bank and Trust.

Bad Word Bully Trap

It is easy but foolish to constantly use foul language for effect or to put others down for sport. If you use curse words when you feel you don't have any better, more creative, or more intelligent way to spice up your message, you are falling into the bad words bully trap. Before long, using such words becomes your default mode, the natural way you speak. Our society has certainly gotten coarser in its choice of language over the years, which is a pity. But bad words highlight ignorance, not power, and bullies are just loud cowards. Like cranking up the volume, bad words only create the illusion of strength. What really lies beneath is weakness.

What's the legacy of being a bad word bully? People will think you're brutish. Brutishness is a bad trait you will have to carry around in your Little Brain baggage.

Good Gossip Tool

You don't always have to refrain from talking about others behind their backs—if you're saying something positive about them. When you speak positively about someone who is not in the room, you not only improve that person's standing in others' minds but also let your listeners know that you are likely to speak well of them when they are not there. You demonstrate that you have goodwill all the time—not just when it benefits you. At the same time, refraining from participating in bad gossip, or even interrupting it and inserting good gossip, strengthens your Me. Those who push for accuracy and honesty gain everyone's respect.

When you use good gossip you begin a chain reaction of goodwill. You can begin to see the impact immediately. Giving compliments behind people's backs is one of the most powerful tools you can use, no matter how big or small your family or organization.

Good gossip travels fast and the impact is stunning. Remember that good gossip must be sincere.

What's the legacy of good gossip? People will think you are classy. You'll deposit a reputation for classiness in the Big Brain Bank and Trust.

Bad Gossip Trap

We may be tempted to engage in gossip and rumor spreading. Doing so can make us feel—briefly and superficially—powerful as we point out people's flaws behind their backs or declare half-truths with authority to make ourselves sound credible and wise. It's a quick way of getting out the message "Everyone else is smaller than me, and I am smarter, more powerful, and more interesting." The catch is that this tactic doesn't work. It only makes people around you feel uneasy and doubt whether they can trust you.

What's the legacy of bad gossip? People will think you are untrustworthy. A reputation of untrustworthiness is something you'll have to carry around in your Little Brain baggage.

A Chinese proverb says, "A bad word whispered will echo a hundred miles." Unfortunately, we've probably all witnessed exactly how this phenomenon can play out in our lives. Consider the following example of the rapid, negative effects of gossip in the workplace in contrast to the positive reinforcement that good gossip can create.

Word Tools and Traps in Action: Coworkers

Angie arrives at work and runs into her coworker Martha on the way to her cubicle.

"Guess what!" Martha tells her. "You know the Wallace contract we just finished? Mr. Wallace called in personally to say it was a pleasure working with you as the team leader, and he'll definitely come back to us next year."

Angie smiles weakly, but she seems distracted.

"Are you okay?" Martha asks. "Aren't you excited to hear that?"

Angie nods. "Sure, I just . . ." She hesitates a moment, then goes on to tell Martha that she just broke up with her boyfriend after discovering that he was cheating.

Later in the week, Martha is in the lunchroom chatting with other coworkers when the department supervisor speaks up.

"Does anyone know if Angie's all right?" he asks. "She doesn't seem like her usual cheerful self today."

Big Brain Response

Martha's Big Brain kicks in and reminds her that Angie probably wants to keep the information she shared private.

"I know she's been working hard on her project," Martha says. "Maybe she's a little tired. But, by the way, did you know that Mr. Wallace was really delighted with her performance and plans to come back next year?"

A few seconds later, Angie walks into the room, and right away, everyone is giving her kudos on the compliments from the big client. Angie's face brightens. As she slips into a seat next to Martha, she whispers to her, "We are trying to work things out." They share a smile.

But what if Martha had not been good in choosing her words and how she used them? What if she paid more attention to impressing the others who were in the room? Here's how the scenario might have played out.

Little Brain Reaction

Martha wants the supervisor to think she's intelligent and that she knows what's going on. Before thinking, she blurts, "She got cheated on by her boyfriend. I feel bad for her—but I *knew* that guy was a jerk."

Only a moment later, Angie enters the lunchroom. Immediately, everyone jumps to offer advice and sympathy.

"It can happen to anyone, Angie," someone says. "Don't be a fool twice!"

Clearly embarrassed, Angie says quietly, "Well, we've decided to try to work things out." She glances at Martha, then quickly looks away, obviously hurt and feeling mistrustful. What is the legacy of Martha's choice of words? She loses Angie's trust, and their close working relationship becomes less productive.

CHAPTER TAKEAWAY

Your ability to choose the right words and to refrain from using the wrong words can save a relationship with a coworker or a loved one. In fact, it can help you reach a new level of friendship and collaboration with all the people in your life.

Control

We know now that the Big Brain is aware, measured, and under control, while the Little Brain overreacts and allows impulse and emotion to rule the moment—basically behaving out of control. But developing the skills to have self-control and to handle others when they do not exercise self-control is no small matter.

Life is filled with moments where a little self-control can make the difference between a friendship beginning to sour or beginning to grow, between a marriage ending or taking on new meaning.

Beyond Patience

More than simple patience, self-control is being aware of the moment and also consciously knowing how to respond at each point in the moment, no matter where it takes you. When you are in control of yourself, all of those in the moment have an opportunity to have a perspective on the situation. One person being in control can act as a benchmark for those beginning to have an out-of-control reaction.

Here are some traps and corresponding tools that will help you navigate the area of opportunity of control.

Staying in Control Tool

When you keep your cool in difficult circumstances, you come from the perspective of "Let's not go crazy here." When you're able to stay calm—or underreact—in tense situations, even in the presence of strong emotions, you have the ability to step back and assess those situations. Instead of reacting to the Little Brain comments of others, assess those comments to help you identify what influences people might be under. Use smiles and friendly words and behavior to defuse the tension.

What's the legacy of staying in control? People will think you are composed. You can deposit a reputation for composure in the Big Brain Bank and Trust.

Overreacting Trap

Overreacting wears a hundred different masks. When you fall into the overreacting trap, you may

- "Kill the messenger": blame the bearer of bad news, whether or not the news has anything to do with the bearer.
- Make poor decisions in haste to showcase your power.
- Take the attitude of "I'll show them" in a conflict or disagreement.
- Get very upset over minor incidents.

What's the legacy of overreacting? Other people will think you are scary. Scariness is a bad trait you'll have to carry around in your Little Brain baggage.

Tolerance Tool

Rather than making snap judgments, you can take the position that everyone has the right to be heard. When you use the tolerance tool, you

- Try to understand the viewpoints of others.
- Listen to all sides completely, even when you disagree.
- Keep your communication channels open and welcoming by asking others for their comments and opinions.

What's the legacy of tolerance? People will think you are fair. Fairness is a good reputation you can deposit in the Big Brain Bank and Trust.

Intolerance Trap

"Intolerance" is not a word that refers to just race, religion, and gender politics. It can apply to any number of interpersonal situations in which someone declares, "It's my way or *no* way." When you fall into the trap of intolerance, you

- Are impatient and never give others a chance to explain.
- Jump to harsh conclusions based on little information.
- Act callously or coldly.
- Disregard other people's feelings.

What's the legacy of intolerance? People will think you are unfair. You'll have to carry a reputation for unfairness around in your Little Brain baggage.

Being Considerate Tool

Being considerate is a simple tool, and all it requires is pausing and taking a moment to not be selfish. You act with consideration when you

- Let others go first.
- Discover the emotional and physical comforts everyone needs in various situations.
- Are fair and share when there is not enough to go around.

What's the legacy of being considerate? People will think you are kind. You can deposit a reputation for kindness in the Big Brain Bank and Trust.

Being Selfish Trap

It's human nature for your personal experiences to feel more important and more central than others' experiences. But that does not mean you have to place yourself first every time. You're being selfish when you take the attitude "I got here first," "I got mine—get your own," or "This is not about me, so I don't care." You demonstrate selfishness when you

- Constantly interrupt others in conversation.
- Say, "Let's talk about something else because this bores me."
- Talk only about yourself and how everything needs to relate to you.

What's the legacy of being selfish? People will think you are greedy. You'll have to carry a reputation for greediness around in your Little Brain baggage.

It's amazing how someone can defuse tension by taking the time to assess a situation and regain control—or notice that others are out of control. Let's look at the example of Quinn.

Control Tools and Traps in Action: A Late Night

Quinn is the head of a production company that has been contracted to produce a theater preview and commercial for a film made by a major motion picture company. At age forty-four,

Quinn has a reputation for being one of the best in the business. On this particular contract, he's working for a movie producer named Jeremy, who's twenty-six. Jeremy is a hotshot and has developed a reputation for abusing his power.

The contract for Jeremy is a big one, and everyone at Quinn's production company has worked hard all week to produce the trailer. It's 9:00 p.m. on the final day, and they've already been through eight major revisions since 6:30 in the morning. They send the eighth and "final" version to Jeremy and wait breathlessly. At 9:30 p.m. the phone rings.

"You know what?" Jeremy tells Quinn on the phone. "I think this last one is not as good as number seven, and number seven was not good enough. What are we going to do? I need this by midnight."

Quinn swallows his annoyance. "Could you hold for one moment, Jeremy?"

"Sure."

Quinn looks at his group of editors, who are all exhausted and at their limit. One of them says, "This guy is nuts! We'll never please him!"

Another steps it up, "Who does that little——think he is?"

And another chimes in, "I'm going to quit."

If Quinn is not careful, the influences of angry editors, long hours, and simple exhaustion could easily lead him to a Little Brain reaction.

Little Brain Reaction

Quinn is frustrated and feels pressured to please his editors. He gets back on the phone and snaps, "Jeremy, I don't know what to think. We tried eight times today, and at this point, we just don't know what to do."

"Well," Jeremy says smugly, "if you can't do the job, just say so. I have twenty other companies in line that want this business."

"Then go ahead and call one!" Quinn slams down the phone. There is momentary glee in the office, and everyone goes home for the evening.

Quinn sits alone at his desk, wondering how he'll ever replace the business he just lost with Jeremy. The next day, in the trade magazine, Jeremy's company announces a new relationship with a rival of Quinn's company.

What is the legacy of that brief moment on the phone between Quinn and Jeremy? Quinn loses a major client and has to lay off two editors.

But Quinn does not give in to the pressure of the moment. He takes control and guides the moment to a very different outcome.

Big Brain Response

Instead of listening to his frustrated editors, Quinn takes a deep breath and regains control of the situation before getting back on the phone with Jeremy.

"Jeremy," Quinn says, "I have truly been impressed with your suggestions today. At this point, I need more of your guidance so I can give you what you want. We're willing to stay here all night to get this done."

The editors groan in the background, but Quinn doesn't let himself get sucked in by their negativity.

"You guys are great, and I know I am not easy," Jeremy replies, his own tone softening. "I think we are close."

Jeremy gives Quinn a few suggestions; then they hang up. Quinn says to his editors, "I know you are tired. If any of you want to leave, I will pick up the slack with no hard feelings." They all decide to stay.

Quinn and his team incorporate Jeremy's ideas, add some of their own, and send off another version of the preview. At 11:45 p.m., Jeremy calls to say, "Congratulations! It's just what I needed."

After the call, everyone sits for a moment, taking in the victory.

Quinn speaks up first. "Ladies and gentleman, today was the day you became the best. It's not about who we're dealing with; it's the product we produce. It's doing whatever it takes."

When Quinn arrives at his office in the morning, he finds an envelope from Jeremy. Inside is a pair of hard-to-get Broadway tickets and a note:

> Quinn,
>
> Please accept my apologies for being such a jerk yesterday. Your crew did a great job, and I just wanted to let you know I appreciate the way you handled things. Enjoy the show.
>
> Jeremy

Quinn's ability to stay in control strengthens his reputation in the industry. He starts pulling in even more contracts, and he is able to hire another editor and grow his business. Not giving in to the pressure of his editors reinforced his leadership.

CHAPTER TAKEAWAY

Developing self-control and the ability to handle others who are not practicing self-control will help you navigate tough moments. The tolerance of others' ideas and comments will give you the perspective necessary in any situation, allowing you to guide the moment to a conclusion that is best for all involved.

Time

O f all the influences in our lives, time seems to be the one we feel we have the least ability to manage. But actually, it is the one we have the *most* control over. In fact, it's an area of opportunity.

Here's how. Time is perfectly consistent. It does not change. Twenty-four hours will always be twenty-four hours. The circumstances that we put ourselves in throughout those twenty-four hours are what change. When we overschedule our lives, we create the circumstances that make time seem as if it is working against us. You need to respect time by planning for enough time to accomplish what you want to accomplish. If you don't plan, you make time your master. Instead of controlling it, time will control you. Time is our friend. It always tells us where we are in relation to it—and it doesn't lie. But how we react to it can have a major impact on our ability to stick with the Big Brain or slip into Little Brain mode. If we pack too many activities into too little time, we get stressed and are far more likely to use our Little Brains. If we let time know how we want to spread out our activities, it will be there, like clockwork, to help us organize. It's a tool when we use it to our advantage—and a major trap when we let it get the best of us.

Don't let time become your master. Control your time. If schedules change, as they tend to do, don't let time be the decision maker. Reset timelines when you need to, and don't allow time to push you into Little Brain mode.

Here are some tools and traps that you need to know about when dealing with issues where time is an opportunity.

Telegraphing Tool

We don't send telegraphs to people anymore, but there are plenty of other ways to send advance notice. Let people know when something is coming up that will affect their lives: a job change, new policies, a major deadline, new rules of the house, and so on. Telegraph anything that takes people out of what is familiar or routine and comfortable to them. This will allow processing time for them to accept the circumstances and make the most of them.

What's the legacy of telegraphing? You will seem diplomatic. Diplomacy is a good trait you can deposit in the Big Brain Bank and Trust.

Ambushing Trap

When you fall into the ambushing trap, you punish yourself and those around you by pushing immediate demands on people who are not expecting them or prepared to handle them. People have little to no processing time to understand what is happening. Ambushes are negative surprises and are not appreciated. You ambush people when you, for example,

- Think that, because you have not planned well and are in a rush, everyone around you should accommodate your needs.

- Impose new rules and send out "effective immediately" and "from now on" memos with little to no warning or discussion.
- Change schedules at the last minute to benefit yourself.

What's the legacy of ambushing? People will think you are deceptive. A reputation for deceptiveness will become part of your Little Brain baggage.

Time Parachutes Tool

When you receive a Little Brain message from someone else, it is always best to wait as long as you can before responding. If you're pressured for a fast response, use time parachute phrases—like a pilot's parachute, they'll get you out of a bind. Here are a few:

- "Let me think about that."
- "I don't know if I have enough time right now."
- "Can you give me some time to consider that?"

When you don't take advantage of time parachutes—you can easily get into "fire, ready, aim" mode.

Before you respond to Little Brain messages from different forms of communication, use these rule-of-thumb wait periods to keep yourself from falling into the trap of speed messaging:

- *Text*—wait ten minutes; your message will be on the other person's phone forever.
- *E-mail*—wait thirty minutes; it will be on the other person's computer forever.
- *Facebook*—wait twenty-four hours; everyone will have it forever.
- *Voice mail*—wait twenty-four hours; it's your voice and it's recorded.

What's the legacy of using time parachutes? People will see you as mature. You'll deposit a reputation for maturity in the Big Brain Bank and Trust.

Speed Messaging Trap

You fall into the trap of speed messaging when you send messages that have not been thought through and you demand a quick response or you react to a message without taking the time to think about your response. For example, you

- Blast emotional e-mails to everyone.
- Send an angry text and expect a fast response.
- Leave voice mails when you are upset.
- Broadcast negative thoughts on Facebook, Twitter, and more.

What's the legacy of speed messaging? You'll seem hotheaded. Hotheadedness is a reputation you have to put in your Little Brain baggage.

Good Timing Tool

A synonym for "good timing" is "tact." You're tactful when you embrace the art of waiting. You choose the optimum time to have an encounter by keeping the legacy in mind. You ask yourself, "Is this the right time to have this discussion?" and recognize that others may not be able to accept the information you have right now. Similarly, you are prepared to take advantage of opportunities when they present themselves. Having the information you need and using it at the right moment makes the encounter successful.

What's the legacy of good timing? People will think you are bright. You can deposit the good quality of being bright in the Big Brain Bank and Trust.

Bad Timing Trap

You can use the right words and the correct tone and even be calm and in control, but if your timing is bad, the encounter itself will leave you wishing you had waited to for a better time to deliver your comments. You fall into the trap of bad timing when you

- Force an issue or question on others because it fits your time schedule—without pausing to ask yourself if it's the right time for them to address it.
- Make even well-meaning suggestions at an insensitive time, such as bringing up someone's unhealthy diet just as he or she is taking a bite of a hamburger.
- Pile on or add to others' anxieties by burdening them with new problems at a difficult time.

What's the legacy of bad timing? You'll seem frustrating to others. Being frustrating is a bad reputation you'll have to carry around in your Little Brain baggage.

Time is an opportunity. But it's so easy to twist time into something that works against you. This happens all too often on the road, when we try to squeeze seconds and minutes out of our day by driving just a little faster, as illustrated in the following story.

Time Tools and Traps in Action: A Moment of Time

Robert is on his way to meet a big client, but he left the house late and traffic is bad. He's racing down the freeway, weaving in and out of traffic. He gets angry at every car in front of him and blames all the other drivers for being slow. As he darts in and out of the various lanes, his anger is growing. He seems to think that everyone is working against his need to hurry and get to the meeting. As he nears his exit, he wants to cut over quickly, but in the next lane, right beside him, is Olivia. Olivia is running a little late on her way to her son's high school graduation. She knows the ceremony is starting soon, and she's eager to get there. Robert tries to cut in front of her, but she feels ambushed by his aggressive driving and does not let him in.

Robert's and Olivia's eyes meet. Robert flips her off and lays on the horn, demanding to be let over.

Little Brain Reaction

Olivia, outraged by his rudeness, speeds up, preventing him from changing lanes. But just at that moment, the car in front of Olivia stops short, and she rear-ends it.

Robert smirks—but the instant he's distracted by Olivia, *he* slams into the car in front of *him.*

Although they are just fender benders, the accidents change the lives of both Robert and Olivia for this day: Robert misses his client meeting and loses a big account. Olivia sits on the side of the road, filling out an accident report. When she realizes she will miss her son's graduation, a tear begins to roll down her cheek.

Big Brain Response

What if Olivia takes a moment after seeing Robert flip her off? She senses that he is in a hurry, being irrational, and acting like a jerk, and instead of taking it personally, she slows down and changes lanes, wanting him out of her vicinity. She realizes that she needs to reset her own time pressure to allow her to be a safer driver.

She continues driving to one of the most important events of her life. As her son crosses the stage, a tear begins to roll down her cheek.

CHAPTER TAKEAWAY

Time is so often misunderstood as an adversary, and when people are under time pressure, their Little Brains are ripe to be activated. But time can be one of our greatest friends when it comes to creating Big Brain moments if we understand how to use it. Telegraph changes and stay away from ambushing people. Time parachutes are always available.

Responsibility

These days, we're constantly presented with examples of dimin-ished personal responsibility, from finger-pointing on Capitol Hill to the blame game on Wall Street. It's almost as if the simple act of stepping forward and saying "I made a mistake" is becom-ing obsolete.

No one is perfect. We will all slip up at some point and create a Little Brain moment. You can easily guide it back to Big Brain ter-ritory if you take responsibility. And in so doing, you'll strengthen your Me and improve your relationships.

Exactly how do you avoid making scapegoats and pointing fingers—actions the Little Brain just can't get enough of? Here are some responsibility tools and traps to point you in the Big Brain direction.

Taking Responsibility Tool

How do you steer clear of blame and instead take responsibility? Learn to enjoy the challenge of solv-ing problems. Do what needs to be done, even when it is not offi-cially your task to perform. Don't be afraid to accept responsibility for actions you've taken and decisions you've made. If someone else is being blamed for your mistake, step up and say, "It's my fault." That way, you will lead others by example. Your response will create legacies that show others the way.

What's the legacy of taking responsibility? You'll seem principled. You will deposit a reputation for principle in the Big Brain Bank and Trust.

Blaming Trap

We've all heard those Little Brain blame phrases a hundred times: "It's not my fault. " "She did it!" "The whole world is against me." "It's somebody else's responsibility." "It's not my job." When people give away responsibility for decision making to others—or blame them for decisions that they already made—they avoid responsibility for the outcome. This trap also pops up when something goes wrong and people are looking for someone to take the fall.

What's the legacy of blaming? People will think you are whiny. You'll have to carry around a reputation for whining in your Little Brain baggage.

Expressed Gratitude Tool

Unexpressed gratitude is like a bucket of water sitting in the sun next to a flower. When the water does not get poured onto the flower, the water evaporates and the flower dies. Instead of holding on to silent appreciation, do your best to practice the Big Brain tool of expressed gratitude. For example, you can

- Express gratitude and tell others what they mean to you.
- Look for ways to give credit to others.
- Find opportunities to highlight your appreciation by giving flowers or small gifts or doing deeds that will be welcomed.

What's the legacy of expressed gratitude? You'll seem gracious. Graciousness is a positive trait you can deposit in the Big Brain Bank and Trust.

Ungratefulness Trap

Egos are sprawling, clumsy items that can sometimes trip over themselves. When something goes wrong, they make sure everyone knows they were never there and had nothing to do with it. But when something goes *right*, they fall all over themselves to make sure their role in the outcome gets broadcast. And they usually fail to acknowledge the many helpers they had along the way.

What's the legacy of ungratefulness? People will think you are vain, and you'll have to carry around a reputation for vanity in your Little Brain baggage.

Apologizing Tool

Apologizing is truly an art form in today's world, but we often resist it with every last fiber of our being. It can be as simple as saying "I screwed up, and I'm sorry." The good news is that *an apology has no expiration date*. When you have done something wrong or just made a mistake, whether in words or in deeds, you must apologize. Healing can begin only when a truly sincere apology has been given, so the faster it comes, the faster the healing begins. But no matter how long it has been, the Big Brain can always find a way to create a positive legacy.

What's the legacy of apologizing? People will think you are sincere. You can deposit a reputation for sincerity in the Big Brain Bank and Trust.

Pouting Trap

Pouting is the ultimate trap of the pessimist. People caught in the trap of pouting say to themselves, whether consciously or unconsciously, "I'm not happy, so nobody is going to be happy." They act resentful when others get more attention or are more successful. They are chronically annoyed and invent injustices to validate their distorted perception of reality. Unfortunately, they can become more comfortable with being annoyed at the world than resolving their problems.

What's the legacy of pouting? People will get tired of the way you seem miserable all the time. A reputation for misery is Little Brain baggage you will have to carry with you.

Taking responsibility is a critical area of opportunity in your life—in your personal and home life as well as in your workplace. The following story shows one example.

Responsibility Tools and Traps in Action: Drama at the Theater

John is foreman for a large construction company. Earlier in the day he was chewed out by his boss because his crew did not finish a driveway on schedule. It was not John's fault the cement truck turned over on the freeway and never arrived, but his boss did not seem to care. John left work frustrated and annoyed.

Tonight John is on his first date with Melanie. They're seeing a movie both of them are excited about, but just before it begins, another couple sits down in the seats right in front of them and starts chatting. The couple continues their conversation even after the movie begins.

Little Brain Reaction

John is getting angry. He was really looking forward to his date with Melanie, and now he can't relax and have a good time. He leans forward and whispers loudly to the couple, "Excuse me, but I paid twenty bucks to hear the *movie*, not *you*."

For a second, the couple falls silent. But quickly, one of them turns around and snaps, "We didn't pay to hear *you* either."

Melanie puts a hand on John's arm, trying to get him to just ignore the comment, but he is furious.

"Look," he shouts, "I said be quiet!"

Immediately, the couple shouts back. The manager of the theater arrives and demands that they all leave. Melanie is mortified and ends her date with John with the words "You really embarrassed me!"

John can't believe Melanie didn't understand his side. He tells himself, "Good. I don't want to be with such an uptight person, anyway."

He never sees her again.

Big Brain Response

As soon as John utters his first words to the other couple, he notices the stricken expression on Melanie's face—the look that says, "What kind of a crazy person am I out with, anyway?"—and immediately takes responsibility for his words. Right after his comment about spending twenty bucks, he backs off and speaks to the couple from his Big Brain, as follows: "I apologize for that comment. It was rude. Please forgive me." The couple also apologizes and they agree to be quiet.

John quietly suggests to his date, "Why don't we find a couple of seats on the other side of the theater? I had a tough day at work today, and I guess I kind of took it out on those people. I hope you'll forgive me."

Melanie is touched by his honesty. After the movie, they end up walking and talking for hours, eventually stopping at a small café. They continue to trade stories and laughter, and by the end of their date, they're mutually enamored. They begin a long relationship—all because John demonstrated through his words, tones, and actions that he was the kind of person who took responsibility for his actions.

CHAPTER TAKEAWAY

Taking responsibility, expressing gratitude, and apologizing and are all parts of everyday living. The more comfortable we are using these tools, the more comfortable our lives will become.

Power

Power—vying for it, allocating it, and wielding it—is an aspect of all levels of human organization, from the family to a country's system of government. The desire for power is a primal human instinct, and it doesn't have to be automatically negative. Of course, we've all experienced or heard about abuses of power, but when you use power appropriately, it can keep people comfortable, keep things running smoothly, and strengthen your Me. Whether power is used positively or negatively, it will have the longest legacy of all the areas of opportunity we've discussed.

The Little Brain finds power elusive. It strives for it, clutches for it, and when it's able to snatch it in little pieces, it gets protective of it and squirrels it away. The Little Brain usually gets power only through someone else or by position; it is not good at commanding power naturally. But it holds on tight to what little power it has—and then gets hungry for more.

Power comes easily to the Big Brain because it isn't looking for power. The Big Brain is most interested in a positive outcome for everyone involved, so it uses the power it has for everyone's benefit. Coincidentally, that tends to bring it more power. The Big Brain gets its power by natural command and respect.

Let's look at the tools and traps of power.

Empowering Others Tool

Empowering others gives you strength. It's possible to lose the argument yet win the moment and the legacy. You are actually far more powerful in an encounter when you have the insight to allow a moment to play out without trying to wrestle for the "win" and allow others to have their moment. When you empower others, you can

- Give them the assistance they need to succeed in the encounter.
- Allow people to make mistakes without taking advantage of their gaffes.
- Support others in their moments and push for a Big Brain legacy.

What's the legacy of empowering others? You will be seen as savvy. You'll deposit their good memory of your savvy in the Big Brain Bank and Trust.

Gullibility Trap

Gullibility is a way of handing power to others. When you are naïve and fail to protect yourself, you can end up in situations that you aren't prepared to handle. If you are easily persuaded by flattery and false compliments or if your need to be liked is more powerful than your common sense, you can find yourself making Little Brain decisions. Sometimes gullibility makes you so fearful of hurting someone's feelings or of being disliked that you ignore danger signs and allow others to push you into situations you aren't comfortable with.

What's the legacy of gullibility? You will look foolish to others. Foolishness is a reputation you'll have to carry around in your Little Brain baggage.

Forgiveness Tool

Learn from the past—but leave it there. Carrying the problems of the past forward is like collecting large rocks on the way up a mountain. Take a look at the rocks you've been carrying and start reframing those memories as lessons rather than injuries. You'll be released from their weight, and you'll move forward more prepared for the future.

What's the legacy of forgiveness? You will seem big. Your reputation for bigness in the Big Brain Bank and Trust will grow.

Holding Grudges and Getting Even Trap

When you hold grudges, you create a little strongbox where you hang on to every minor injustice. At any given time, you can pull one out and spring it on someone as "ammunition." You can use lots of little tricks to convince yourself that you have a right to settle the score with others. You can tell yourself, "Once I get them back, I'll be happy" or "After I get even, I can let this go." Punishing people makes the Little Brain feel powerful—for the moment—but it also starts a vicious cycle of Little Brain activities.

What's the legacy of holding grudges? People will remember that you are vengeful. You'll have to carry around a reputation of vengefulness in your Little Brain baggage.

Good Farewell Tool

The farewell is the last chance you will have while still in the moment to leave a Big Brain legacy. When you use the good farewell tool, you actively seek ways to end an encounter on a positive note. All those involved will look forward to seeing you again. You might say, for example,

- "I appreciate the conversation. Thanks for listening."
- "Looking forward to next time."
- "Thank you."

What's the legacy of a good farewell? People will find being with you enjoyable. You will deposit a reputation of enjoyability in the Big Brain Bank and Trust.

The Last Word Trap

When you are always trying to get the last word in a conversation or encounter, you fall into the last word trap. If you are unable to let a moment end on someone else's joke or clever comment, you may end the encounter with some cynical cliché, such as "Like anyone cares" or "Don't hold your breath" or one of the hundreds of other such Little Brain finishes you can give to an encounter. You feel the need to be the last to speak because you think the person who speaks last wins the moment.

What's the legacy of the last word trap? People will remember that you are snide. You'll have to carry snideness in your Little Brain baggage.

Let's look at an example of how easy it is to fall into a power trap in the workplace, where power is so rigidly structured.

Power Tools and Traps in Action: Power Trips and Falls

Lara is a secretary at a large advertising firm. She is always on time—but today, circumstances took over, as they inevitably do. She missed her bus and is running late. She was supposed to get to work early to set up the conference room with beverages and snacks for an important meeting, but by the time she arrives, the meeting is already under way. She walks quietly into the back of the conference room and begins to set things up.

Big Brain Response

Lara finishes setting up and is on her way out the door of the conference room when her boss speaks up. "Just a moment, Lara," he says. "Everyone, I want you to meet Lara. She is one of our best and most valuable people. She is the reason we can get everything done around here. Thank you, Lara."

Lara smiles proudly and exits the room.

When she gets back to her desk, she is feeling very appreciated. She knows her boss did that to make her feel better about being late. Her phone rings. It's a longtime friend who tells her about a job opening at a company closer to her home. She tells her friend thanks but says she is happy where she is: "I like the people here."

The legacy? Lara stays right where she is and grows with the company, even though it's further from home.

How could her boss have used power differently to create a different legacy? Let's change his response.

Little Brain Reaction

Lara finishes setting up and is on her way out the door of the conference room when her boss interrupts the meeting to say, "Lara, I was really hoping the room would have been set up when we got here."

Everyone at the conference table turns and looks at Lara.

"I'm sorry I was late," she tells everyone in the room. "It won't happen again."

"That's okay," her boss replies. "We knew you would *eventually* make it."

Lara slips out of the room, embarrassed.

After Lara leaves, the boss blurts out, "You've got to keep them on their toes."

When she gets back to her desk, Lara is feeling tremendously unappreciated. She has never been thanked for the many times she has been early or stayed late, but the one time she arrives late, she has to apologize in front of everyone. Her phone rings. It's a longtime friend who tells her about a job opening at a company closer to her home. She tells her friend to set up an interview.

The legacy? Lara, a well-trained, valuable employee, leaves the company and has to be replaced. She tells the story of that morning for the next year.

CHAPTER TAKEAWAY

Power used properly can create wonderful moments, but when it's misused or wasted on getting even or for personal gain, it can work against you. Your power to affect the lives of others will have the longest legacy of all.

Your Legacy Bank
and Baggage

As we put all of these moments together, we begin to see the big picture of how these legacies add up. Let's take a look at the potential bank accounts and the potential baggage that may have been created.

Everyone has a Big Brain Bank and Trust, and everyone carries Little Brain baggage. At this point, we've seen how the seven areas of

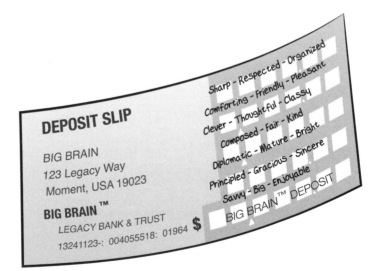

Figure 23.1 Your Big Brain legacy bank account

opportunity—awareness, tone, words, control, time, responsibility, and power—can either add to your bank or add to your baggage.

As you begin to choose Big Brain responses more often, your account could include a reputation for classiness, thoughtfulness, maturity, cleverness, friendliness, and more. Figure 23.1 can help you picture this.

Now let's look at all the potential Little Brain baggage that could have been packed away. In your Little Brain baggage, you could be lugging around a reputation of immaturity, greediness, whining, unfairness, and more. Figure 23.2 shows what this might look like.

Figure 23.2 Your Little Brain baggage

That's a lot to carry!

The good news is that despite all that Little Brain baggage, every encounter will give you a chance to remove some baggage and make a deposit to your Big Brain Legacy Bank.

Your Little Brain baggage and Big Brain deposits can be different with different people. You may have immaturity, deceptiveness, and carelessness baggage with one person and frustration, whining, and foolishness baggage with someone else.

In your Big Brain bank account you could have sharpness, classiness, and leadership with someone. Or you could have brightness, maturity and pleasantness with someone else.

Mixed Legacies

You could even have some Big Brain and some Little Brain baggage with the same person. You could have cleverness, hotheadedness, and fear as your legacy with someone. Or you could have immaturity, foolishness, and kindness.

The only way to lighten your load is to remove the Little Brain legacy in each specific area of opportunity with each person—and replace it with a Big Brain deposit. The next time you encounter that person, you might choose to offer an apology or a clarification. Or you might simply demonstrate your use of a Big Brain tool instead of falling into a Little Brain trap so that this new moment can move some baggage out and create a new legacy.

What's Your Legacy?

What do you want that legacy to be? Think of the different people in your life. What is your legacy with each of them? Was your last moment with a person a Big Brain moment or a Little Brain moment? Do you have baggage to remove?

In your personal life, your relationships with your family members and close friends will bear the legacies of your encounters.

In your business life, your relationships with your customers, coworkers, clients, and leaders will bear the legacies of your interactions.

CHAPTER TAKEAWAY

Businesses spend millions and millions every year trying to bring in new customers, define their images, promote their brands, and improve their legacies in customers' minds. All that money spent is of little value unless the people in front of the customers know how to connect with them and know how to handle themselves in every encounter.

PART FOUR

Applying the Seven Principles of Big Brain Communication

As these pages bring our moment to a close, many new moments are about to open. In the time it has taken to read this book, you have already learned how to look at every encounter a little differently. You have learned how to make the most of the moments in front of you.

Going forward, try to leave each moment on a positive note, follow up, be clear, and get comfortable with apologizing, forgiving, and empowering people. Before you know it, your Big Brain will be at the helm of each conversation, each encounter, each moment, your job, your career, your relationships, and your whole life.

Now we'll take a look at the seven principles of Big Brain communication. You'll learn how to apply the Big Brain/Little Brain concept to every situation in your business life and your personal life.

The seven principles are as follows:

1. Stay aware of the legacy of the moment.
2. Keep your Big Brain in control.
3. Choose the correct tone.
4. Choose the correct words.
5. Choose the right time.
6. Accept responsibility.
7. Use power wisely.

These seven principles have the proven ability to elevate your communication skills and therefore your success in life because, ultimately, everything boils down to the quality of your communication. At the end of this part of the book, you'll find a list of the principles that you can put where you will see it every day. When you apply the seven principles in every encounter, you will be amazed at the positive changes that result.

THE FIRST PRINCIPLE

Stay Aware of the Legacy of the Moment

Sometimes we can read a book that inspires us to take specific actions, or we can attend a seminar that leaves us with an enthusiastic feeling about going forward. But then, reality hits in the form of a crisis at work or a challenging situation at home, and before we know it, we've gone back to our old ways of thinking and reacting.

That's why awareness is so important. Throughout the day, throughout the week, throughout the year, keep the *encounter, moment,* and *legacy* concepts at the forefront of your mind. Reinforce these same concepts in appropriate, helpful ways with the people around you so that they can stay in Big Brain mode, too.

Get into Big Brain Mode

At Disney's theme parks, the last thing a cast member sees before heading into the park is his or her own image! Mirrors are posted in every backstage area right by the passageway that leads to the section of the park where the guests can be found. This gives the cast members one last chance to make sure that they look appropriate, that their uniforms or costumes are in place, and so on.

As important as it is for us to maintain professional images when we prepare to meet the public, it's even more important that we have our minds in the right place, focused on and aware of the Big Brain and Little Brain, moments, and legacies, the three keys to this methodology. So if you don't have a mirror to look into as you leave the house, you may want to put up a reminder to stay in Big Brain mode, just to keep that awareness alive.

"Have a Big Brain Day" may sound a little corny, but focus is the key to awareness, so find a phrase that can remind you to stay aware. It's not corny if it works.

Before you go into any encounter with anyone—a family member, a team member, a client, a customer, anyone at all—always ask yourself what you want from the encounter. Don't let the legacy be an accident. Plan for the legacy, and that will guarantee positive moments in the encounter.

Big Brain Push-ups

As an exercise, take a look at your calendar from last week. Identify the moments that stick out in your mind, whether they were positive or negative. What is the ratio of Big Brain moments and Big Brain legacies to Little Brain moments and Little Brain legacies? If you aren't happy with how you handled some of those moments, what could you have done differently? Do you need to do any follow-up?

Now look at next week's schedule. Every get-together is an encounter. How can you best ensure that the moments in your encounters will turn into Big Brain legacies? Which upcoming moments are likely to start or possibly end in Little Brain legacies, given the people with whom you're meeting or the subject matter of those meetings? What can you anticipate to help keep Little Brain away?

Where Are You Today?

Next, try to identify the influences present and acting on you today. What mode are your influences in?

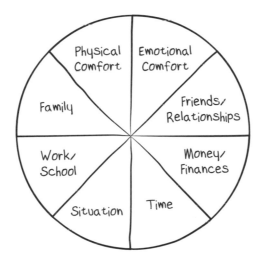

Figure 24.1 Your Circle of Influences

Look at your own Circle of Influences as shown in figure 24.1. Each of these influences can be in Big Brain or in Little Brain. In what mode are the following?

Emotional comfort influences	Big Brain or Little Brain
Physical comfort influences	Big Brain or Little Brain
Family influences	Big Brain or Little Brain
Friendship or relationship influences	Big Brain or Little Brain
Money or financial influences	Big Brain or Little Brain
Work or school influences	Big Brain or Little Brain
Time influences	Big Brain or Little Brain
Situational influences	Big Brain or Little Brain

What about Me?

Finally, once you know what influences are affecting you, you can take a look at your Me. Is it a strong Me or a weak Me? Are any major issues affecting it? What major influences are potentially harming your Me?

CHAPTER TAKEAWAY

Awareness is key. When you are aware, you have the freedom to opt for the Big Brain way of operating in the world. That creates great moments. Great moments create great legacies. And it all starts with awareness. Try to know the influences that are present. And always keep the legacy of the moment in mind.

25

THE SECOND PRINCIPLE

Keep Your Big Brain in Control

Psychologists make a distinction between reacting to situations and responding to them. *Reacting* happens when we act on reflex without hitting the pause button long enough to think through whether the reaction is appropriate. All too often, reactions have Little Brain written all over them. We speak without thinking, we act without considering the consequences of our actions, and we—and our friends and family members—pay the price. *Responding*, by contrast, implies taking the time to think through just what our answer should be.

Look back on moments when you or others around you showed the ability to remain in control in tough situations. Take the time to think about the different stages of your life and remember the times when self-control was your friend. Now take a moment to think back to last time you lost control. What were the circumstances that set you off? Who or what pushed your buttons? What influences were present?

Little Brain Buttons

It's hard to stay calm when provoked. And yet we know that in order to be successful, we must remain calm—calm in the face of challenging personalities, calm in the face of challenging circumstances, calm regardless of what comes our way.

No one expects you to be perfect, so don't even try. Just take the time to identify the things that you know will push your Little Brain buttons. Do particular people activate your Little Brain when they enter a room? Do you know that certain situations on the road will activate your Little Brain? Think of your home environment. What are the Little Brain buttons there: a messy room, lights left on, or trash that needs to be taken out? Do the same for your work environment. Once you have identified these known Little Brain activators, get proactive. Find ways to prevent them from occurring, but while you are in that process, don't let your Little Brain make a big deal about them.

As Thomas Jefferson said, "When angry, count to ten before you speak. If very angry, count to one hundred." It doesn't hurt to do a little counting, but what's most important is to count on your Big Brain to carry you through those moments when a Little Brain answer would turn a small problem into a big one.

You can find a worksheet for identifying Little Brain buttons at BigBrain.com. This worksheet will allow you to look at your different environments and find Little Brain activators in each one.

Overreacting Does the Most Damage

If reacting is what we seek to avoid, overreacting clearly is worse. Overreacting is what happens when we become so emotionally upset by a situation, a set of facts, a provocation, or some other set of circumstances that we just can't think straight.

Overreacting in the business world leads to loss—loss of income, loss of responsibilities, loss of prestige, and sometimes loss of your job.

Overreacting at home creates divisions that can last for years if not addressed. Often relationships will have a difficult time recovering from recurring overreacting.

How Do You Maintain Control?

Ignoring a problem is not the answer, and overreacting creates its own set of problems. So the sweet spot becomes responding—thinking through appropriate actions to take, or words to say, in order to resolve a situation. When you are in control, you can eliminate problems before they have a chance to fester.

Getting rid of selfishness is another key to keeping the Big Brain in control. Selfish reactions to circumstances cloud our vision and do not allow us to recognize the opportunities right in front of us.

Zig Ziglar speaks about the concept of heaven and hell as banquets. In hell, there's a lot of wonderful food on the table, but nobody's eating because the forks and spoons are way too long for any individual to eat with. In heaven, the banquet looks exactly the same—except that everybody's having a great time because everyone's using those long utensils to feed the person on the opposite side of the table! Which banquet do you want to attend?

CHAPTER TAKEAWAY

Don't let your Little Brain do the talking. In other words, stay in control and take time to think before you say or do anything. Respond instead of react.

THE THIRD PRINCIPLE

Choose the Correct *Tone*

We pick up bad tones like we pick up bad habits. The tones stick around, waiting to be used by the Little Brain at will.

Fortunately, good tones are also a part of our habits, but the struggle is to make sure the Big Brain tones win the race to the comment that is about to be made. Compassionate, caring, and calm tones will serve you well in any communication. Remember these three Cs and your communication will take on tones people will want to be around.

Some other basic tones are serious, disappointed, excited, grateful, friendly, delighted, and welcoming. You can find a list of tones to fit any circumstances at BigBrain.com.

Anchor Tone

Before any encounter that you know is coming, identify the anchor tone you want to use for that encounter. The anchor tone is your central tone for the conversation. Calm is a good basic anchor tone. In a serious conversation, you may want to add a tone of seriousness or even a tone of concern. In a lighthearted situation, you may want to add a fun tone.

Whichever tone you choose, remember that if you have an anchor tone, no matter how crazy or out of hand the situation gets, you can always come back to your anchor tone to reset the direction of the encounter. This way, even if others are losing perspective, you won't lose yours. (Write your anchor tone on something you can see and keep it close.) And your ability to keep your tone constant will give perspective to others. Whatever happens, don't chase the tones of others. Choose your anchor tone and stick to it.

If your tone gets out of control, the subject of the discussion is forgotten, and instead of the focus being on the actual issue, it turns to how you need to make the other person feel better about how you said something. At this point you need to spend time to eliminate the negative emotions caused by the tone you used. This is a recipe for disaster in any relationship.

Going Up? Going Down?

Escalators and elevators are great in malls. They take shoppers from one level of stores to another with ease. In conversations, though, tone escalation can be an outright negative.

Many of us have a tendency to get louder and louder when we are not getting our way. The problem is that even if you "win" an argument with someone by using loudness, you often still lose the moment. Maybe you proved that you were right and the other person was wrong, but all you've really done is driven that person away from you.

Choosing a Big Brain tone all the time takes practice. But your ability to use the correct tone will begin to make your life smoother, easier, and more pleasant.

Ready for Your Closeup?

Sometimes we have a positive message to offer but our words don't align with our facial expressions.

In some retail stores, the first person you see is the security guard, a menacing presence whose job it is to make sure that nobody steals anything from the store. This situation is not very welcoming. By contrast, in other stores and in restaurants, an employee gives you a warm smile as soon as you arrive, as if that person is your host. When you greet people, what is the tone of your face: security guard or host?

What Is the Tone of Your E-mails?

Establishing and maintaining an appropriate tone is even trickier in digital or written communication, especially e-mails and texts. As we discussed earlier in the book, electronic messages may be terrific for sharing specific pieces of information, but when it comes to conveying tone, they can be disasters waiting to happen. It's become very common to communicate with people close to us in the short, choppy, unemotional, and flat tones of the digital world. These toneless communications are no replacement for your voice and your presence.

Have you ever taken a look at the e-mails or texts you send? Take a moment to see how you "speak" in the digital world. If the typos don't scare you, the tone quality should.

When you're looking at your written communications, see how many did or did not have a proper greeting and salutation. A warm salutation creates a sense of rapport and respect.

As an exercise, sort through the digital communications that you've sent in the last couple of months. Create two folders on your desktop—a Big Brain folder and a Little Brain folder—and put all the messages that came from your Big Brain or your Little Brain into the appropriate folder. Which folder is bigger? Do you need to do any follow-up? Do the same with messages you have received.

Checking Your Tone

Think back to the most recent situations in which you've been involved in a dispute. Who escalated the tone? If it was you, was that necessary? Was your Big Brain or your Little Brain at work?

If it was the other person, did you keep your cool when you responded? Or did you escalate your tone as soon as the other person did? We all have fallen into that trap.

When we sit down at a computer or pick up a smart phone or other device for the purpose of texting or sending messages, our Little Brain seems to get activated more. We can pay a very high price for failing to maintain Big Brain standards in all communications, and it doesn't take that much effort to move from Little Brain to Big Brain mode in the tone of any form of communication, oral or written.

CHAPTER TAKEAWAY

Tone is the message. Before an encounter, choose the tone you will use to anchor your message. Remember that compassionate, caring, and calm tones will serve you well in any kind of communication.

Choose the Correct Words

I remember a wonderful episode of *I Love Lucy*, where Lucy hires an English tutor to teach Ricky, the Mertzes, and herself the fine points of elegant speech.

"There are two words you must never use," the specialist warns her. "One of these is *swell*, and the other one is *lousy*."

"Okay, what are they?" Lucy asks.

"One of them is *swell*, and the other one is *lousy*," the tutor repeats.

"Well give us the lousy one first," Fred Mertz says.

It's a funny moment on a classic show, but the problem is that all too often, we can choose words that undermine ourselves and the image we seek to create.

Most of us don't use words like "swell" or "lousy" anymore. Instead, many swear words have become accepted parts of normal, everyday conversation. Even a generation ago, people in "polite society" never used obscenities in the course of their day-to-day conversations. But today, society is much less polite. I'm often surprised to see individuals who are in positions of power and influence giving little thought to how they speak.

Finding Replacement Words

Here's the challenge: Can you eliminate from your vocabulary any unacceptable language or ugly words? Can you come up with replacement words that take the obscenity and profanity out of the mix and in the process make others around you comfortable as you laugh at the sound of those words?

You could start a contest with friends and family members to see who can come up with the best replacement words for the typical ugly words and profanity that litter our verbal landscape. The winner could even receive a T-shirt with all the new words on it. You have a responsibility to set an example and begin to eliminate profanity from your vocabulary.

Little Brain Letting Off Steam

If you hit your hand with a hammer by accident, it will hurt, and letting go of four-letter words is probably the least of your concerns at the moment. If you are by yourself when something happens that normally would set off a series of expletives, no problem. It may actually be healthy to let it out and let it out loud. But if you are not alone, if you are with people you care about or people you are responsible for, using foul language leaves a poor legacy. You can still let off steam—just choose different words when others are present.

Good Gossip Improves Morale

A simple way to describe the idea of saying something nice about people behind their backs is "good gossip." Good gossip is spreading good news about the people around you, celebrating their accomplishments, and letting others know what they have done when those people are not present. Doing this has some long-lasting benefits. It lets the people you are with know you will make good comments about them when they are not there. In addition, good gossip is one of the most effective tools to bring people to a place where they will begin to listen to you more. It makes them want to listen closer to what you are saying.

Planting the Seeds of Recognition

Start by noticing when you use someone's name. It's a great opportunity to check the comments you are about to make. Recognize that the person whose name you utter will eventually hear everything you are about to say. Then, identify the number of times you used a name today—were the comments that followed positive or negative?

Somehow, everybody hears about each other's shortcomings and failures. We need to spend more time consciously getting the word out about the successes of the people in our lives. Whatever we pay attention to will naturally grow. So if we're paying attention to the good things people do, more good things will happen.

And Then There Is "*You*"

No word is more personal than "you." When "you" comes out of your mouth, it's best if it is followed by a compliment. Before using the worn-out clichés of "you always," "you never," "you better," "you have to," and other comments where "you" is used as an attack word, take a moment to see if the Little Brain is in control of the conversation.

CHAPTER TAKEAWAY

The words you use matter. If you have the habit of using profanity, improve your vocabulary. Find new words to replace the ugly ones. And remember to use good gossip to celebrate the accomplishments of others. You always have a choice.

Choose the Right Time

There's a time and a place for everything. It's poor timing to tell someone about a crucial meeting the day of the event. It's good timing for parents to speak to their daughter about boys long before her first date.

Similarly, you don't want to deliver bad news to people while they are in front of others. An astute leader of a family or an organization is courteous enough to take someone aside and privately deliver whatever criticism needs to be expressed. By contrast, good news ought to be broadcast to everyone immediately. Let others celebrate the victory of one of their peers. In that situation, everybody wins.

The Telegraph Is Still Working

On some occasions you must inform those close to you of impending change. So what's the best, most effective way to do it? As we saw in chapter 20, the answer is telegraphing. Telegraphing means conveying important information *in advance of the change.* There's a huge difference between saying "From now on, we will do things differently" (which doesn't give people enough time to assimilate the change) and saying something like "Starting in two weeks, we will need to do things differently." Telegraphing empowers people to adapt to a change on their own terms. It gives them processing time.

Telegraphing involves the art of seeing what event, circumstance, happening, or occurrence is coming up and letting people know about it with enough time to process and accept the change. It may be an upcoming family event, a discussion on cutting expenses, or a new job or position that requires your schedule to change. It's anything new.

No One Likes to Be Ambushed

Anything sudden can activate Little Brain reactions. A key human need is to process change in a healthy manner. So be sure to telegraph change to people instead of springing change on them. See what happens when you make the shift away from ambushing them with "from now on" to telegraphing "in two weeks."

Consider also the fact that most people are not fond of surprises—and for good reason. We're all creatures of habit, and we don't like our habits disrupted, especially when they're disrupted suddenly.

We've all been in the position, however, when we felt ambushed. Perhaps we were given a message at a wrong time or place. We might have been embarrassed by the presence of others who heard a criticism or angry that we were not given time to formulate a response. Ambushing doesn't build character. It builds resentments, and it can activate anyone's Little Brain because it does not allow time for a Big Brain response. Choosing the right time to deliver a message is just as important as choosing the right tone and the right words with which to share that message.

The opening and closing minute of every encounter is a great time to smile and say hello or good-bye to people. It is not a good time to jump at people with comments about overdue tasks that need to be performed or ask them for answers they are not expecting to give.

The Closing Minute at Home

When people are leaving for work or school in the morning, it can be a tense moment. Getting last-minute items and feeling the pressure to be on time creates a moment that is not good for serious discussions about household issues or even about things that have been on your mind. Let the last minute walking out the door from the house be a moment of support.

The Opening Minute at Work

Walking in the door at work is the opening encounter of your business day. This opening moment sets the tone for the entire day. This is the time to say hello and greet others. If you walk by people without greeting them, you send a message of not wanting to be bothered. Take this minute to acknowledge others and then get on with the business of the day. At the same time, when you see others walking in to work, give them a minute to get settled. This is not a good time to pile on the tasks that need to be done or the messages that have to be answered.

The Closing Minute at Work

The end of a long day when people are leaving is the closing encounter of the workday. It is a time to finish the day on a upbeat note and send people home thinking positive thoughts about their work. While someone is walking out the door is not the time to spring major business questions on them that require a thought-out response. Pushing people at the end of the day for important answers can activate the Little Brain. It creates an unnecessary time pressure regarding issues that could have been dealt with earlier or can wait until tomorrow.

The Opening Minute at Home

The minute people walk in the door from a long day at work or school may not be the best time to start asking questions that you have been waiting to get answered or to discuss items that have been on your mind all day. Give people the first minute to set things down and get settled. Open with "Hello" instead of "I need to talk to you." Use the first minute to reconnect and recognize that this is the opening encounter of the evening at home.

The Oops Principle

When you are writing a letter by hand, you can always look at it and say, "Oops, that is not what I should say." Then you can erase it and rewrite your message. In the digital realm, once the message is sent, there is no chance to erase it. There is no Oops button that can bring back a message that is gone.

Given the velocity of messages coming at us in so many forms, it's all too natural and understandable to go into speed messaging mode. However, when we do, we aren't taking the time to consider that each of these messages constitutes a moment and will create a legacy, for better or for worse.

Reacting quickly rather than responding is a setup for disastrous speed messaging. It's caused when someone sends you a message by text, e-mail, voice mail, or other method and you think you have to respond *immediately*. When you are in speed-messaging mode, you often react to messages without adequate thought and concern. You may send messages you would have been better advised to keep as thoughts to yourself.

So stop feeling as though you've got to toss back every one of those messages with a prompt response, as if you were a professional juggler that can't let any item hit the floor. Instead of hitting the Send button, hit the Pause button.

Time Parachutes Create Soft Landings

Not every question requires an immediate answer. Not every communication requires an immediate reply.

At times, an issue can seem like the most critical matter in the history of the universe, and the perception by some will be that it demands immediate action. In reality, not every decision must be made *now*. As we have seen, you can use a time parachute, which is a phrase that gives you a chance to jump out of an uncomfortable situation and give yourself time to consider an appropriate response. For example, it's hard to argue with a time parachute like "Give me some time to think about it" or "Can I ponder that for a while?" or even "I'm not ready to answer that at the moment." Using a time parachute has a calming effect on all involved. Some decisions really do need to be made immediately—but most can wait a little.

The legendary UCLA basketball coach John Wooden used to tell his players "Be quick, but don't hurry." It's a subtle distinction and a very meaningful one. We've all got to be quick today. We have to keep up with the ever-increasing pace of the world around us, and we've always got to be at the top of our game. Hurrying, however, is counterproductive and makes us sloppy.

Rather than choosing from a list of standardized time parachutes, it's best if you use ones that sound natural coming from your lips. What's the right message at this time for you to send, in your own words, that can defuse a seeming crisis and give all involved enough time to consider the matter rationally? Write down three time parachutes of your own that you feel comfortable using and keep this list close.

The great philosopher Unknown once said, "We usually learn less from victory than from defeat." So don't be afraid to look back at some of the moments of your past. What are the situations where you might have exercised less-than-perfect timing? What are the decisions that you wish you could have back? What could you have handled differently in the past, and how can you improve your decision-making skills going forward?

CHAPTER TAKEAWAY

Timing matters. Don't ambush others with important news at the last minute or make big changes without giving people time to process the change. And when someone tries to ambush you, use a time parachute to ensure a soft landing. Be sure to pause before you hit the Send button.

THE SIXTH PRINCIPLE

Accept Responsibility

The blame game: it has a million participants, and it never has any winners. You know how it goes. Something goes wrong. And before long, many explanations are put forth as to why it is someone else's mistake and the situation devolves into who is better at finger-pointing and denial of responsibility.

Is It Safe to Take Responsibility?

The flip side of dishing out blame is accepting responsibility. Accepting personal responsibility has virtually disappeared. It's all too easy—and accepted—to blame our choices, and the results we get from our choices, on anything or anyone else. Much has been written about how our culture has all but destroyed the concept of personal responsibility and what a great toll that has taken on our society. As a result, today when someone actually does feel responsible for his or her actions and takes responsibility for them, that person stands out from the crowd. Someone like this can achieve the highest levels of success because, in the end, people have the most trust in someone who can admit mistakes. So what about you? What are some of the examples in your experience where you have taken responsibility for your actions?

It's time to honor yourself (privately) and others (publicly) for the moments when you and they stepped up and did what was necessary, whether they were accepting responsibility or simply handling a task that no one else wanted to touch.

What You Are Grateful for Grows

One of the themes of these seven communication principles is the concept of recognizing individuals for the contributions they make. Do you foster an attitude of gratitude? Do people close to you believe that you're going to "catch" them when they do something right and not just when they do something wrong? We wouldn't stay in a relationship for long with someone who wasn't grateful for our efforts. And it's not enough just to be grateful—we have to show that gratitude. Which people close to you have helped you at times and may even have helped to create your success? Have they received the acknowledgment and recognition they deserve? Who deserves a little more recognition for their efforts?

Make a list, and it should be a long list. Begin to find ways to express your gratitude to these individuals. After all, none of us succeed alone. And remember, there is no expiration date on the expression of gratitude, no "statute of limitations." Even if something happened years ago, if it hasn't been recognized, there's no better time than right now.

There Is No Expiration Date on Apologies

Take a moment to look around at all the people in your life. Can you identify incidents that occurred or comments that were made in the past that might deserve an apology?

Remember that perfection is unattainable, so you don't have to hold yourself to an impossible standard. But don't settle for lower standards than you know you can attain.

We all make mistakes. We all say the wrong thing once in a while. We will all slip into Little Brain mode from time to time. But only the courageous among us take the time to rise above mediocrity and apologize when an apology is appropriate.

An apology, heartfelt and sincerely made, can go a long way toward repairing damage you may have consciously or unconsciously caused.

CHAPTER TAKEAWAY

Everyone makes mistakes. When it's your turn to fall short, take responsibility instead of trying to find someone to blame. Make a sincere apology when you need to. Recognize others when they do well. Show your gratitude and appreciation.

Use Power Wisely

B ill Gates said, "As we look ahead into the next century, leaders will be those who empower others." Empowering others by supporting them, giving them room to be themselves, allowing them to make mistakes, and shepherding them when needed will ultimately bring you the power to accomplish what you desire.

The principle of using power wisely ties together the concepts of power and forgiveness. So often we think of power strictly in terms of who has the power and who doesn't. We all have some level of power. Power is the most potent when it is shared. True power is never needing to show you have it.

For example, any discussion or conversation has moments when you will begin to notice that this is not your argument to win, that winning the argument will not be productive. Often, letting others win the point or the argument can work to your benefit. It will not always be easy, but allow it to happen. Let others win some points in the encounter, and let them shine a little. Save your victories for when the issues are significant, and be ready to let someone else have the spotlight.

Power Can Work for You or against You

Power can be used to enhance people's lives personally and professionally, and it can also be used to harm them in both arenas.

If power is used to help people grow, learn, and become more productive, it will have a positive legacy.

It can also be used for negative purposes. One particularly destructive use is holding a grudge. Holding grudges against people gives them enormous power over you. You are allowing them to occupy space rent-free in your brain. You are letting them be far too important to you, and you are failing to ask the critical question, How important was the event that caused the grudge? Are you aware of any grudges taking up space in your head?

Can Forgiving Someone Really Bring Peace?

Seek opportunities to let go of old grudges.

If you know someone whom you have not forgiven for any reason, take a moment and recognize how much of a distraction this grudge holding is to you. Even if you are not ready to walk up to the person and express forgiveness today, silently forgive him or her, and let the negative power begin to dissipate. Eventually you will have the strength to let the person know that you no longer hold a grudge and have moved on.

Think of clients or old friends you don't talk to anymore. Do you see opportunities here for you? Do you no longer see certain people because of something that happened long ago? Could it be beneficial to rekindle those relationships?

Authors who write about the connection between spirituality and prosperity make the point that when we are not succeeding in life, it's because we have failed to forgive someone from our past who needs forgiving. Just as we have made mistakes and expect forgiveness, others have done the same and deserve the same.

No matter how long a wound has been open, the forgiveness you provide will always be appreciated. Ultimately, failing to forgive others creates an invisible anvil around your own neck.

CHAPTER TAKEAWAY

We all have some kind of power. Empowering others is a way to empower ourselves. Sometimes it's better to share power by giving others a chance to shine. Don't give away your power by holding a grudge. Forgiveness will release your burden and increase your personal power. The power is always yours.

The Seven Principles of Big Brain Communication

1. **Stay *Aware* of the Legacy of the Moment.**
   Identify the influences that are present.

2. **Keep Your Big Brain in *Control*.**
   Don't let the Little Brain do the talking.

3. **Choose the Correct *Tone*.**
   Remember: the tone is the message.

4. **Choose the Correct *Words*.**
   Improve your vocabulary.

5. **Choose the Right *Time*.**
   Don't force the issue.

6. **Accept *Responsibility*.**
   Don't blame others.

7. **Use *Power* Wisely.**
   Don't give yours away.

AFTERWORD

Dear Reader,

Let's continue this conversation at BigBrain.com.

You are now ready to begin a new chapter in your life—a chapter where you are in control of your responses and where you know how to deal with the way others react.

Let me know how this book has affected your life. Write to me and tell me how it is working for you.

Tell me about your Big Brain moments and your Little Brain moments. I would also like to hear about the Big Brain and Little Brain moments of other people that you may observe throughout your life.

Be a part of helping others identify Little Brain activity wherever you see it. You can also show others what Big Brain moments look like to you.

Thank you for giving me your time. Most of all, thank you for sharing this moment with me.

Have a
Big Brain
Day ™

Sincerely,
Kevin T. McCarney
Kevin@bigbrain.com

INDEX

amusement park story, 51–52
anchor tone, 152–153
anger responses, 129–131
apologies, 81, 82, 128, 167–168
appreciation, 136, 137
arguments, 74, 75–76
attacks, 73–74, 75–76, 90–91
attitude changes, 75
awareness, 88
  Big Brain push-ups, 146
  counter encounters story, 93–94
  getting into Big Brain mode,
    145–148
  for keeping perspective, 95
  of legacy of the moment, 145, 148
  not taking it personally, 90–91
  taking it personally trap, 91
  tools for, 89–90
  unawareness trap, 90

baggage, 82, 84–85, 88, 139–140.
  See also legacies; traps
banquets in heaven and hell story,
  151
baseball game story, 19–21
Big Brain
  activators of, 21
  awareness push-ups, 146
  control of, 7

creating positive moments with,
  17, 87–88
during conversations, 56–59
examples of (*see* tools)
finishing touches on encounters,
  80–81
functions of, 9, 11
getting into Big Brain mode,
  145–148
influences on, 28, 29–31
legacies of (*see* legacies)
location of, 9–11
moments, 51, 52
principles of, 143–144, 172
technological tools and (*see*
  technological tools for
  communication)
tones of, 98, 102–103
word choices, 105
bigness, 134
blame, 126–127, 166–167
brush-offs, 81–82

calm communication, 152–153
career influences, 23, 24–25,
  30
career moments, 14–15
change management, 160–161
choices, 30–31, 34, 82

Circle of Influences, 147
impacts of, 25–27
on a bad day, 35
with Big Brain and Little Brain, 23
in the moment, 30–31
clarifications, 81, 82
cleverness, 106
cluelessness, 90
comments, 50–51
communication
learning/understanding language, 96–98
mistakes in, 101–103
principles of Big Brain, 143–144, 172
speed communicating, 67
technology and (*see* technological tools for communication)
three Cs of, 152
tone of written, 154–155
See also conversations; tone
communication brains, 8, 9–11, 77–78. *See also* Big Brain; Little Brain
complaints, 93–94
composure, 113
conscious responses, 73–74, 79
consciousness of moments, 85
consideration of others, 114–115
control by Big Brain/Little Brain story, 7–8. *See also* self-control
controlling the moment, 75, 143
conversations
elements of good, 55
give and take in, 56–59
lying in wait during, 63
managing multiple (*see* managing multiple moments)
opportunities for memorable moments in, 60
problems of, 55–56
See also communication
coworkers story, 110–111
customer encounters, 14–15, 45–46, 92, 141

defeats and victories, 164
dental hygienist story, 29–31
digital technology. *See* technological tools for communication
discouraging word story, 78–79
Disney theme parks, 145–146
drama at the theater story, 129–131
driving angry story, 123–124

e-mail communication, 65–66, 154
emotional comfort/discomfort, 23–24, 27, 30, 147
Enchilada Story, 1–3, 26–27
encounters
Big Brain finishing touches, 80–81
creating positive moments in, 45–46
first and last minutes of, 162–163
follow-ups to, 81, 82, 146
Galarraga story, 46–47
influences on actions during, 22–23
as opportunities, 48
parts of, 43–44
quality of your, 4
successful, 92
See also moments
enjoyability, 135
everyday moments, 12–13

Facebook/social media sites, 69–71
facial expressions, 99, 100, 154
fairness, 113, 114
feedback, 14–15
finishing touches, 80–81
follow-ups to encounters, 81, 82, 146
foolishness, 133
forgiveness, 47, 81, 82, 170
front-line staff, 14–15

Galarraga, Armando, 46–47
Gates, Bill, 169
getting even, 134
gossip, 56–59, 60, 78, 108–109, 157–158
graciousness, 128

gratitude, 127–129, 167
greediness, 115
grudges, 134
guitar teacher story, 38–40

honesty, 130

image, 141, 145–146
influences
    awareness of, 27, 78, 146–147
    on Big Brain, 29–31
    career, 24–25
    choice of response to, 30–31
    circle of (*see* Circle of Influences)
    definition of, 22
    during encounters, 22–23
    failure to recognize, 90
    financial, 24–25
    on interactions, 28
    on Little Brain, 29–31
    major impacts on your Me by,
        33–34
    on moments, 74–75
    personal self's, 32
    primal, 23–25
    situational, 25
    types of, 30, 147
    unseen, 3
    on your Me, 147–148
kindness, 115

late arrival story, 75–76
leaders, methods of strong, 19
legacies
    ambushing, 121
    of anticipating, 92
    apologizing, 128
    assuring positive, 80–81
    of assuming, 92
    of awareness, 90
    bad gossip, 109
    bad timing, 123
    bad word bully trap, 108
    baseball game example, 19–21
    being considerate, 115
    Big Brain (in general), 18–19, 83

blaming, 127
calmness, 99
creating negative and positive,
    17–18, 85, 136, 137
    in customers' minds, 141
discouraging word story, 78–79
empowering others, 133
escalation, 99
example of, 47
expressed gratitude, 128
forgiveness, 134
good farewells, 135
good gossip, 109
good timing, 123
good words tool, 108
gullibility, 133
having the last word, 135
hello and good-bye tool, 100
holding grudges, 134
intolerance, 114
knowing wanted, 94
Little Brain (in general), 84–85
    of loss of control, 117
mixed, 140
negative facial expression, 100
not taking it personally, 91
positive facial expression, 99
pouting, 129
selfishness, 115
speed messaging, 122
staying in control, 113, 118
taking it personally, 91
taking responsibility, 127, 131
telegraphing, 120
tolerance, 114
ungratefulness, 128
using time parachutes, 122
of word choice, 111
Legacy Bank and Trust deposits,
    84
    added baggage, 88
    being principled, 127
    bigness, 134
    brightness, 123
    classiness, 109
    cleverness, 106

Legacy Bank and Trust deposits, (*continued*)
  composure, 113
  diplomacy, 120
  enjoyability, 135
  fairness, 113
  feelings of comfort in others, 99
  graciousness, 128
  kindness, 115
  maturity, 122
  organization skills, 92
  pleasantness, 100
  potential baggage, 139–140
  potential deposits, 138–139
  respect, 91
  savvy, 133
  sharpness, 90
  sincerity, 128
  thoughtfulness, 108
life circumstances, 25
listening, 55, 63. *See also* conversations
Little Brain
  activators of, 21, 150
  baggage of, 84–85
  behavior of others using, 51–52
  brush-offs by, 81–82
  control of, 7
  during conversations, 56–59
  examples of (*see* traps)
  functions of, 9, 11
  influences on, 28, 29–31
  keeping Little Brain away, 146
  legacies of (*see* legacies)
  life-changing moments by, 122
  location of, 9–11
  other people's use of, 76
  receiving Little Brain messages from others, 121–122
  sneak moments by, 79
  someone else's, 50–51
  technological tools and (*see* technological tools for communication)

  tones of, 97, 103
  word choices, 105
Little League teams, 18–19

managing multiple moments, 68–69, 72
maturity, 122
Me
  awareness of strong/weak, 41
  core senses of self, 32–33
  influences on, 33–34, 147–148
  strength of your, 34–37, 47
  weaknesses of your, 33–34, 38–40
miscommunication, 62
misery, 129
mission of successful businesses, 15
mistakes, 128, 168
mixed legacies, 140
moment of time story, 123–124
moments
  Big Brain, 51
  career, 14–15
  creating, 16
  during conversations (*see* conversations)
  encountering (*see* encounters)
  everyday, 12–13
  legacy of, 143
  Little Brain, 50–51
  managing multiple, 68–69, 72
  mopping, 15–16
  negative, 81–82
  positive, 17, 146
  power of daily, 49–50
  quality of, 53
  recognizing Big Brain, 52
  recognizing/identifying opportunities in, 87–88
  in relationships, 13
  staying in Big Brain mode, 66

mopping moments, 15–16
morale, 157–158
motivation, 22

movie company story, 115–118
multitasking. *See* managing multiple
    moments

obscenities, 156
oops principle, 163
outcomes
    awareness of, 3
    broadcasting, 128
    changing, 75, 117
    determining, 96
    negative, 92
    positive, 1, 132
    responsibility for, 127

patience, 112
people skills, 18
perfect game story, 46–47
performance when no one is watch-
    ing, 15–16
person-to-person communication,
    65
personal life legacies, 140
physical comfort/discomfort, 23, 26,
    30, 147
physical cues, 100
positive facial expression, 99
positive messages, 105–106
Powell, Colin, 16
power, 88, 143
    benefits and problems of, 169–
        170
    desire for, 132
    effects of, 137
    empowering others tool, 133, 171
    forgiveness tool, 134
    good farewell tool, 134–135
    gullibility trap, 133
    holding grudges and getting even
        trap, 134
    last word trap, 135
    power trips and falls story,
        135–137
    of words, 105

primal influences, 30
principles, 127
profanity, 156, 157–159
public relations company story,
    63–66
push-ups, Big Brain, 146

reactions/responses
    Big Brain and Little Brain, 12, 23,
        25–26
    choosing to respond, 151
    consciously choosing, 79
    differences between, 149
    Enchilada Story, 1–3, 26–27
    to feedback, 14–15
    overreacting, 113, 150
    spring-loaded, 105–107
    taking time before, 121–122, 150,
        163
    See also tools; traps
recognition, 158, 167
relationships
    communication skills and, 62
    conversations for developing
        (*see* conversations)
    influences on, 30, 147
    moments in, 13
    people skills for good, 18
    as surrounding influences, 24
reputation. *See* Legacy Bank and Trust
    deposits
responsibility, 88, 143
    apologizing tool and, 128
    blaming trap and, 127
    comfort with taking, 131
    drama at the theater story, 129–
        131
    expressed gratitude tool and,
        127–129
    pouting trap and, 129
    safety in taking, 166–167
    taking responsibility tool and,
        126–127
    ungratefulness trap and, 128

savvy, 133
self, core senses of, 32–33. *See also*
    Me
self-control, 88
    being considerate tool, 114–115
    being selfish trap, 115
    how to maintain, 151
    intolerance trap, 114
    late night story, 115–118
    others' lack of, 118
    overreacting trap, 113
    remaining calm, 149–150
    skills for self-control, 112
    staying in control tool, 113
    tolerance tool, 114
    of your tone, 153
self-esteem, 32
selfishness, 115, 151
senses of self. *See* Me
sharpness, 90
sincerity, 128
situational influences, 30
speed communicating, 67
strength through empowerment, 133
tact, 122
technological tools for communica-
    tion, 59, 61
    e-mail communication, 65–66,
        154
    listening and, 63
    miscommunication with, 62
    oops principle, 163
    speed-messaging trap, 122
    taking time before responding,
        121–122
    texting, 63–66, 68–69, 70–71,
        100–101, 154, 155, 163
    thinking before sending messages,
        66
    tone of e-mails/texts, 154–155
tension defusers, 113, 115
texting, 63–66, 68–69, 70–71,
    100–101, 154, 155, 163
time, 88, 143
    ambushing trap, 120–121, 161

bad timing trap, 123
    closing minutes, 162
    controlling versus being controlled
        by, 119–120
    creating Big Brain moments, 125
    good timing tool, 122–123
    influences of, 30, 147
    moment of time story, 123–124
    oops principle, 163
    opening minutes, 162–163
    speed-messaging trap, 122
    taking time to respond, 163–164
    telegraphing tool, 120, 160–161
    time parachutes tool, 121–122
timing, 160, 164, 165
tone, 88, 143
    anchor tone, 152–153
    calmness of, 98–99
    checking your, 154–155
    escalation trap, 99
    facial expressions and, 99
    hello and good-bye tool, 100
    lesson from daughter story,
        101–103
    loudness, 153
    as the message, 155
    positive messages through,
        153–154
    recognition/understanding of,
        96–98
    setting/resetting, 103
    three Cs of communication, 152
    in written communication, 100–101,
        154
    See also communication
tools
    anticipating tool, 91–92
    apologizing tool, 128
    awareness tool, 89–90
    being considerate tool, 114–115
    calmness tool, 98–99, 149–150
    empowering others tool, 133, 171
    expressed gratitude tool, 127–129
    forgiveness tool, 134
    good farewell tool, 134–135

good gossip tool, 108–109,
  157–158
good timing tool, 122–123
good words tool, 107–108
hello and good-bye tool, 100
late night story, 115–117
opportunities for picking up, 88
spring-loaded response tool,
  105–106
staying in control, 113
taking responsibility tool, 126–127
technological (*see* technological
tools for communication)
telegraphing tool, 120, 161
time parachutes tool, 121–122,
  163–164
tolerance tool, 114, 118
traps
  ambushing trap, 120–121, 161
  assuming trap, 92
  bad gossip trap, 109
  bad timing trap, 123
  bad word bully trap, 108
  being selfish trap, 115
  blaming trap, 127
  escalation trap, 99
  gullibility trap, 133
  holding grudges and getting even
    trap, 134
  intolerance trap, 114
  last word trap, 135
  late night story, 115–118
  opportunities for falling into, 88
  overreacting trap, 113, 150
  pouting trap, 129
  speed messaging trap, 122

spring-loaded response trap,
  105–107
taking it personally trap, 91
unawareness trap, 90, 93
ungratefulness trap, 128
trust, 83, 84–85, 109

unfairness, 114

vanity, 128
vengefulness, 134
victories and defeats, 164

Wooden, John, 164
words, 88, 143
  "you," 158
  bad gossip trap, 109
  bad word bully trap, 108
  choosing what, when, and how
    to use, 104–105, 111, 157
  coworkers story, 110–111
  good gossip tool, 108–109
  good words tool, 107–108
  I Love Lucy story, 156
  improving vocabulary, 159
  replacements for unacceptable, 157
workplace, 14–15, 69–70, 147
written communications
  e-mail communication, 65–66,
    154
  texting, 63–66, 68–69, 70–71,
    100–101, 154, 155, 163
  See also technological tools for
  communication

Ziglar, Zig, 151

ACKNOWLEDGMENTS

Editors, editors, editors. A book does not become a book without editors. "Writing a book is like building a house: you have to start with the foundation before you can build the walls." Wise words from a wise woman, Sharon Goldinger. Thank you to Sharon and her editors, who were instrumental in helping me craft this book into its final form.

There are as many people to thank as there are pages in this book, and each one of them played a part in bringing *The Secrets of Successful Communication* to life. I would like to thank a few of them here.

My brother, John, whose constant conversations and clear thinking over many years helped me focus on the message I wanted to get out. Gig Kyriacou and David Golden, who challenged me to go faster as we did our evening exercise walks and, while walking, challenged me on every aspect of the book.

Jeff Russell and Susan Wooley, for their encouragement when I first introduced to them to the book. Don Riddell, for his kind words and leadership. Harald Herrmann of Yard House restaurants, who gave me great feedback and great conversations on the subjects in this book. Steve Supowitz, for the many lunches and long discussions about the ideas here.

Russell Kamalski and Kristin Loberg, for great guidance in steering me in the right direction when the book was in a very raw state. Larry Walsh and JRW, for keen insights and inspiring words when I really needed them. Dr. Mark Pierce, for his invaluable vote of confidence in the material. Nancy Pierce, PhD, whose insights and comments added a unique perspective.

Ryan McCarney, for adding his youthful perspective and taking apart every page and asking great questions. My sisters, Maureen, Eileen, Sandy, and Sharon. My brothers, Dennis, John, Jerry, and Pat.

Jon Melichar, who read the rough draft and came back with words of inspiration.

Barry Samson, whose comments on writing style were right on target.

. Emilio Urioste, whose Big Brain leadership as principal of a very large high school is still inspiring me. Stan Carrizosa, who will no doubt be giving me lessons on Big Brain leadership for a long time.

Steve Schindler, a fellow author, for providing his intuition on how to put the material together, and Jerry Wade, Kevin Ary, and Keith Stevens for their quiet intelligence that was always present.

Ben and Chelsea Holcomb, for countless debates on the subjects at hand and amazing comments. Blakey St. John, for the many early morning breakfasts to fine-tune some of the concepts in the book.

Raul Porto, for constantly demonstrating the Big Brain way to respond in any situation. Kevin Holland, a man who shows strength and Big Brain decision making to others in his own way.

Steve Bishart, who spent so many hours with me having coffee late into the evening and on into the morning to help me with the formatting and the message. Donovan Moye, for the hundreds of art-related outputs.

Skip Moye, mother in-law extraordinaire. My lifelong friends who have been and will always be there: Tamara Farr, Joe Miceli, Lita Villiacana, Gary Greenberg, Peter Hubbard, Mike Goodrich, Jackie Hines, Joe Bayless, Peter Pergelides, John Sangmeister, Brad Waisbren.

My Big Brain mentors, Frank Lutz, Fran Schwengel, Bill Crookston, Zack Rozio, Ted Alben, Phyllis Truby, Mike Parker, Sam Young, and Candice Moore, who demonstrate Big Brain leadership daily.

Patty Reveles and Ingrid Martini, who saw "Big Brain vs. Little Brain" in its infancy and watched it grow into something that others could use.

Richard Sheppard and Ben Holcomb, for their illustrations. Beverly Butterfield, for her interior design, and Sam Kuo, for his everlasting patience as we set a record for the number of cover design samples.

To all whom I have yet to mention, thank you.

ABOUT THE AUTHOR

Businessman, entrepreneur, and community leader Kevin T. McCarney has had millions of encounters with people of all kinds since he opened his first Poquito Más restaurant in 1984. From the beginning, he has worked to create a business that would inspire loyalty from both his customers and his employees. He understands that a business thrives with every great encounter and suffers with every poor one. And he believes that the same is true of every part of life.

That first small restaurant has grown into a $15 million-a-year business with twelve locations in the Los Angeles area, including one on the lot of Warner Bros Studios, serving over 4,000 customers every day. Based in Burbank, California, the restaurants specialize in fresh Mexican food. Because each restaurant produces over 900 tortillas a day, Kevin invented an aluminum tortilla press, a machine on which he now holds multiple patents.

Kevin has been a guest speaker at the USC Marshall School of Business, the UCLA Anderson School of Business, and Woodbury University. He has served on the board of directors of the California State Compensation Insurance Fund, the California Restaurant Association, the Burbank Arts in Education Foundation, the Boys and Girls Club of Burbank, and the Universal City-North Hollywood Chamber of Commerce.

Kevin has been encountering customers since his first paper route at the age of seven. Growing up in Hollywood, California, he worked as a janitor, a waiter, a manager, a trainer, a switchboard operator, a doorman at Grauman's Chinese Theater, and a tour guide at Universal Studios. He currently lives in Burbank, California, with his wife Nina and daughters Katelyn and Grace.

Please visit www.bigbrain.com for the latest news about Kevin McCarney as well as contact information regarding his availability to speak to your organization.